SCANDAL!

CHRISTINE KEELER

Scandal!

Xanadu

TO MY SONS

British Library Cataloguing in Publication Data

Keeler, Christine
  Scandal!
  1. Great Britain. Politics. Scandals, 1960–1969.
  Biographies
  I. Title
  941.085′6′0924

  ISBN 0–947761–75–6

First edition

First published in 1989 by Xanadu Publications Limited
19 Cornwall Road, London N4 4PH

Typeset, printed and bound in Great Britain by
Richard Clay Ltd, Bungay, Suffolk

CONTENTS

PHOTOGRAPHS

1. Me by the pool at Cliveden, where it all began.
2. Stephen Ward in a relaxed moment.
3. Mandy Rice-Davies leaving the Old Bailey.
4. John Profumo and his wife Valerie Hobson.
5. Eugene Ivanov in his Russian naval uniform.
6. Lucky Gordon trying to get at me outside the Old Bailey.
7. Joanne Whalley as me in the film *Scandal!*
8. Me reading the Government version. Justice?!?

PREFACE

HERE IS the truth at last! It's a relief finally to be able to tell it, because every time I've tried to publish my story it has been rewritten by journalists, or completely invented.

Some will consider it a shocking tale, but I make no apology for the way I lived my life when I was young: if I had been a man, people would no doubt say, 'He was a bit of a lad, wasn't he?', but when a girl behaves like that she's a tramp – or worse. This is true even now, when we are supposed to be much more liberated. Add a couple of high-ranking politicians and you have the ingredients for what has been called The Scandal of the Century!

It all happened a long time ago, but it just won't go away. In the last couple of years there have been new books (mostly by journalists) trying to explain exactly what was happening with Profumo, Ivanov, Stephen Ward and MI5 – and no doubt the idea of making money out of us has been a factor too. But I have not helped with any of these books, and each time I read a new one I think right away: 'No, you've got it all *wrong!*' This is not surprising, as I am really the only person who now knows what did happen.

I get fed up, too, with newspapers portraying me as some kind of tragic, bitter victim, when all I've been trying to do for the last twenty-odd years is live quietly and bring up my family. There *were* major injustices, of course, but for the survivors life does go on – and it doesn't have to be in a Tel Aviv nightclub, either.

Now there's a film, too: *Scandal!* I did help with that: Palace Productions bought the rights to *Nothing But* by Sandy Fawkes and myself, and I spent hours with them going over the events of the so-called Profumo Affair, so that every detail would be right. It brought that period vividly back into my mind, and the research we did helped to fill in some background information that had become blurred over the years, which has helped me to get all the details right in this new book. The only thing I can't guarantee is that every conversation is word-perfect – obviously, no one has total recall, but I preferred to try and capture people's real voices, and I am sure that the gist of what they said *is* correct.

It was also exciting to visit the film-set and meet the actors and actresses, the writers and directors, and the crew. I spent quite a bit of time with Joanne Whalley, who plays me in the film, and the rest of the cast were friendly and interesting: John Hurt plays my good friend Stephen Ward, and Ian McKellen is Jack Profumo.

It's strange to have a movie made about yourself. As this book goes to the printer I haven't seen the film, but I hope it finally does justice to the people who suffered in 1963, especially Stephen.

– CHRISTINE KEELER
World's End, 1988

1

PRISON

THERE HAD been a time when I wanted only to stand at Speakers' Corner and confront those crowds of pig-eyed, pot-bellied men and their frustrated, thin-lipped wives.

'Look at me! Yes, YES! Isn't it exciting? Here I am – Christine Keeler, *News of the World* for *The People*. I take one *Mail*, two *Mirrors*, three *Observers*, a *New Statesman* every week and any number of *Times*.'

Thank God, I never had the opportunity to discover whether the crowd would have turned away in shame or whether they would have hurled stones at my naked flesh and trampled the tattered ribbons of muscle into the mud.

The same fleshy faces that had swarmed me at Heathrow, hoping to catch a glimpse of SEX, now pressed closer, leaving smears of sweat and saliva on the window of the cab that was taking me to spend my nine-month sentence in Holloway Prison. I watched them, feeling nothing but sorrow that they couldn't think of a better way of spending an afternoon.

After I had been sentenced, I felt only relief that it was all over and that I would be shut away in a small, black cell far from public scrutiny, where I might find some peace. The publicity had come to dominate my life. Standing in the dock, all I knew, or wanted to know, was that I was going to prison for six months. Everything else had become a muddle, but prison was safe. Prison was sleep and food and forgetting. Prison, Mother Prison, meant time for me to think, to see and to understand.

'Why don't you cry, Christine?' my solicitor had asked, with all the warmth he possessed.

'I can't, I just can't. I'm so pleased to know that I can at least see the end of it all. Just six months and it will all be over. My life will be my own again.'

'No, it's not that easy,' he warned. 'What you'll find in six months time is that you are just beginning to feel the effects of the past two years.'

I didn't understand him then – I don't think I could have. It was easier to dismiss him, to think he was being silly.

* * * * *

They marched me through the wing to chanted abuse from prostitutes and mad women. Slowly they banged their tin mugs as I walked by. Bang, bang, bang. My God, what place was this I had come to? I didn't know it would be like this. But I didn't cry. I held my head high and with every muscle in my body rigid, I walked forward.

I spent that first night in the prison hospital. The next day they took me to the first offenders' wing where girls were kept for a fortnight before being transferred to an open prison. The 'screw' they put in charge of me for the first few days never left me alone for a moment. It was hell. I was given a job in the library, where of course all the inmates could come and stare at me.

My screw took me for the usual blood test and bustled me to the front of the queue of women, which instantly singled me out as a favourite. The same thing happened with the VD test, fingerprint test and the photographs.

When they informed me I was going to have an IQ test, it just about finished me. They had taken over my body, but I was determined they weren't going to get my mind. I mucked up the test, so they sent me to see the psychiatrist.

'Why don't you want to take the test?' she asked.

I ignored her.

'You're think you're smart, don't you? Think you've got a big name. But look at yourself. You're not a bit smart. You've got yourself into prison, that's all.'

I hadn't cried since the crowds had jeered at me in the streets for weeping during the trials. Now I ran hysterically out of the room.

'What's happening? I don't know what's happening?' I screamed.

The psychiatrist fetched me back.

'I had to be cruel, to make you break,' she tried to explain. In the end I took the IQ test and passed with flying colours.

'People with high IQ's,' the psychiatrist told me afterwards, 'are likely to crack under the strain of being in prison. I suggest that you try and concentrate your mind on something useful. Take up a new subject, a hobby.'

I decided to take up Spanish, and ended up having lessons twice a week with Joan Bakewell. I also asked if I could be transferred from the library because I couldn't stand being stared at. Instead, I found myself scrubbing floors in my own wing.

'Get down properly on your knees, Keeler.' They told me, but I went on squatting.

After my fortnight in Holloway, there was talk about me being transferred to an open prison.

'She'll run away,' my mother told the Governor.

'She'll run away,' echoed the solicitor. And I would have run away. My stepfather was very ill and I wanted to see him. But they kept me in Holloway, and I was transferred to making shirts in the workroom. It was very dull, but what can you expect in prison? At least it provided a routine. I worked for hours looking forward to the next five-minute break. Then worked again, longing to get back to my cell to count the days until my release, making quite sure that there really were ninety days more, not eighty-nine.

They put me in the 'dungeons' twice. The first time it wasn't my fault. The scissors had just been collected in the sewing room, and the wing officers had come to take us for exercise. Usually when the scissors had been collected we were allowed to wander about freely. On this occasion, I was chatting away when one of the screws shouted.

'Keeler!'

I turned round to look at her. It was the fat forty-year-old with dyed blond hair and bright lipstick. She had had it in for me for some time.

'Go and sit down.'

'The scissors have been collected,' I said, and turned away to carry on chatting.

'I'll put you on Report, if you don't sit down,' she bawled. I ignored the old bitch and out came the notebook. Report meant being sent to the dungeons. First offenders hardly ever go on report. Whilst I was in Holloway, first offenders had come and gone, a series of new faces, but not one had ever gone on report.

I waited in the dungeon until the Governor was ready to see me. It was a bare room with nothing but a mattress on the floor. Eventually I was marched through the centre of the prison to the Governor's office. You're supposed to have your head suitably bowed, but mine wasn't. The Governor sat at her desk whilst five screws stood there, one on either side of the Governor, one on either side of me, plus the bitch who reported me.

'I asked this prisoner to go and sit down and she would not,' the workroom screw broke out. 'And she replied . . .' I couldn't hear what she said, but judging by the looks on the other screws' faces, she must have said that I swore at her.

The Governor looked at me. 'Have you anything to say?'

'All I said was that the scissors had been collected,' I replied and waited. That was it. They fined me a shilling off my weekly four shillings and five pence, but the screw who had booked me docked my money down to two shillings and eleven pence for three weeks. I got so fed up with her in the end that I asked for a transfer back to scrubbing the floors. At least that was peaceful. The doctor agreed to the transfer back to my own wing where I was also given the job of looking after the budgies.

I loved those birds. I used to spend a couple of hours in with them every day. One had a bald chest and pecked, but that didn't bother me. They became the centre of my life and the screws never seemed to mind if I locked myself in with the birds.

At free times I read Steinbeck and Zola novels from the library and at weekends, when we were allowed to do what we wanted, I used to work in the garden. I liked keeping myself busy. One day one of the Red Bands, the girls the screws think they can trust, handed me a note containing ten cigarettes. I thought at first she was making a pass at me. A lot of that went on. The lesbian screws always asked to be transferred to the borstal wing where the impressionable fifteen-year-olds were kept. After release, some of the girls tried to get straight back into the prison, because they had a more exciting life inside.

But my note was from a male prisoner who had been painting the roof of our prison. He had written 'I think you're the greatest in the world.' After being locked up for four months the merest approach from any man was enough to send me flying passionately in love with him. I started combing my hair and going out on exercise. Eventually I wrote back:

'Hi – I think you're great. Are you married? If not, why don't you give me your phone number so I can ring you when I get out. Love, Chris.' I sent the note to him at four o'clock in the afternoon by another Red Band. The next morning I was on Report again. Down to the dungeons – eugh! – and up in front of the Governor.

'A certain note addressed to you, Christine, from a male prisoner, has been handed in by a warden. It was discovered lying on the floor.'

I didn't believe her for a moment, then realised that the Red Band had handed it in. I had three days remission stopped. Three days didn't bother me unduly. Three days on top of six and a half months seemed like nothing, but all the same I was determined not to let it happen again. I had been warned that the next time I got into trouble I would probably get two weeks remission stopped, and that would have been just too much.

When the time came for me to leave, the Governor made secret plans to get me out of prison without the press catching sight of me. The Principal Officer was upset that I was leaving. She was hated by many of the girls and had even been thrown over the balcony in the borstal wing. She was extremely strict, but to my mind any harshness was made up for by her fairness. Most screws have their favourites, and I suppose I might have been hers, though I never took advantage of this. She acted tough, but underneath she was as soft as my own mother.

'Keeler, I am Lawson,' she said, and I would reply with a cheeky grin, but not without respect:

14

'Lawson, I am Keeler and with your brains and my looks we could become great partners in crime.'

She actually came to the prison on her day off to say goodbye to me.

'Keeler, I want to say that I hope you're going to get on all right.'

'Thank you, Miss Lawson.' I told her I thought she was a wonderful officer. 'If only there were more officers like you.' I actually felt tears welling inside me, so I escaped to my cell to cry for a few minutes before I was finally released.

I stepped outside the gates of Holloway, afraid to lift my eyes from the dust at my feet. It seemed that Stephen's ashes were clinging to the soles of my shoes. Remembering the destruction for which I was blamed made my scalp tingle. Imaginary voices whispered, 'Whore, prostitute, pervert.'

My solicitor met me at the gates and drove me fast through the streets to a bungalow that he had rented by the seaside, where my parents were waiting for me. There were so many cars on the roads and people driving them. People walking across the streets, people buying things, wheeling their children in prams and pushchairs, laughing and crying. Horrible, terrifying people again. I shuddered. I didn't want to know. Just for a moment I needed the budgies and the screws and the endless floors to scrub. The scrubbing brush and pail, tin mugs and the other prisoners. The ones you like, the ones you ignore, the ones you dislike. The good screws, the bad screws – the lot. But more than that I wanted to see my parents outside prison, in a house with a carpet and an oven and all sorts of ordinary things.

I was afraid of the apologies, of the guilt. I would have to say, 'I'm sorry I've let you down,' feeling all along that

15

it wasn't my fault, but that I still had to apologise, to excuse something that I couldn't have stopped.

At last the moment came. I put my arms around my mother.

'Hello Mum. Hello Dad. How are you? Not a bad little bungalow is it?' I said, trying to sound ordinary, keeping the conversation to everyday matters. We went to see *Tom Jones* at the cinema. My solicitor had brought me a blond wig so that no one would recognise me. I enjoyed the film, even though I was terrified of all the people around me. When we were leaving, I thought that they were all staring at me. It must have been that blond wig.

That night my mother stayed with me and I sat in front of the mirror to have a look at myself.

'Oh, Mum! I'll never be the same again. I'll always have to wear a wig.' I pulled the damn thing off in a fury and flung it on the floor. 'What's happened to me, Mum?' She came over to me, to comfort me, crying too.

'Never mind, darling. We'll get over it,' she said quietly. Something inside me leaped, and I pushed her roughly away. Close human contact terrified and revolted me.

'Don't touch me! Don't touch me!' I screamed at her. I didn't want to hurt her, but I was so torn inside, the hate I felt for myself was too much to bear. My mother cried all night whilst I remained stonily silent. I didn't have it in me to comfort her. The hate I felt inside was too great for me to be able to give or accept sympathy.

We returned to London after a few days to face the inevitable.

'I think we should have a press conference,' my solicitor advised. 'And then we'll get it all over and done with in one go.'

I agreed, trusting his opinion, though I loathed the idea. We went back to the house that had been bought for me

16

during my imprisonment. I had never seen it, although I had owned it for eight months or more.

There they all were, the press animals – just as they had been before I went to prison. It seemed as though the nightmare was beginning all over again. They were allowed to take photographs and ask their questions. Thank God for Mr Lyons, who answered their queries and sent them away in no time at all. In my opinion the reporters were the Devil's disciples, and I wouldn't even raise my eyes to look any one of them in the face. I just thought to myself, 'I hate all of you for what you have done to me.'

* * * * *

My mother and I got a call one day from a man called John Lewis, a thoroughly nasty piece of work. But for his meddling, Stephen Ward might still have been alive. John Lewis invited us to have a drink with him. There seemed no harm in it, but no sooner had we entered the room than he started digging up the past.

'You know, of course, that I had an affair with your daughter.' He looked my mother straight in the eye. I was stunned and wondered what on earth my mother could be thinking.

'That's a lie,' I shouted, but he just grinned. 'It's a lie. Honestly, Mum. He's lying. When is it all going to end?'

My mother defended me.

'I don't want to hear anything about my daughter,' she said proudly. 'Come on, Christine. Let's go.'

We left, my mother still carrying on at him as we went out of the door.

'You're a rude, dishonourable man. Can't you under-stand that Christine has been through enough already? She doesn't need your kind of talk.'

In prison my dreams had been distorted and tortured by the violent angry scenes I had been through, by the greedy faces pushing nearer and nearer, getting at me, forcing me to believe in the twisted morals they called truth. I doubted now that the nightmares would ever end.

2

WRAYSBURY

My EARLIEST memory is of a hospital visit. My hand above my head, held by Mum as I tottered through the ward to visit a man lying in bed with his tummy bandaged up. He was my father. Later, after he was well, he left us.

Before my stepfather arrived, I lived with Mum and Granddad and Nan, with Betty and Pam – my mother's half-sisters, but they were much younger than Mum. Pam was two years older than me, and Bet was even younger. My step-Granddad had a large, bald head and worked on the railways. He was terribly fussy about being clean. On Saturdays he sat the three of us little girls on the table and scrubbed us down, then he'd scrub the whole house down while Nan didn't do much except shout at him and moan at us all.

Then Mum met a man, and told me that I was to call him Dad. Pam, Betty and I fought for his affection. He played with us a lot and gave us half a crown when we were good.

One day we left Nan's and went to live with my new father beside the river at Wraysbury. Dad, as I soon called him, converted two old railway carriages into a sort of caravan for us. I had my own room for the first time, instead of sharing with Mum, so I slept with my little knitted lamb for company. There were only three caravans in Wraysbury; everyone else lived in bungalows.

A girl called Anne, a year and a half older than I was, lived two doors away. One day, when I was five, I fell into the river and Anne jumped in and saved me. I was very proud.

'She's my best friend,' I told Mum, 'because she saved my life.' Anne was the only other girl of my age in the area, so most of the time I played with the boys. We usually went to the river. Once we found an unexploded wartime bomb and carried it all the way back to one of the boy's homes. Every time we dropped it, we ran away and waited for the explosion. Eventually we hauled it up before the boy's dad. The boy stood there, his hands on his hips, grinning.

'Look what we've found, Dad.' His father went white and sent us all packing. The RAF evacuated the whole area and took the bomb away, but we got our names in the local paper for digging it out of the mud and slime.

Dad was strict. He gave me a patch of garden to work at, the worst piece. I hated doing it. Dad was determined to bring me up tough, and never let me get away with being just a girl. There was the time Anne hit me; she often did, and I didn't do anything about it because she was older and bigger than me. I used to run back indoors to my Mum, crying.

'Mum. Mum. Anne's hit me. She hit me,' and of course I'd get all Mum's sympathy and attention. But once my Dad was at home, he wasn't going to let me off that easily. He told me:

'Shut your face crying and just get straight along outside and hit her back, or you'll find yourself in worse trouble with a good hiding from me!'

I did exactly as he said, and after that Anne never dared to hit me again, but we did have to put up with her Mum who came round straight away.

20

'Your Christine's hit my Anne,' she shouted. 'And just look at the state of her.' She pulled Anne forward by the arm to show my Mum how her nose was bleeding.

'Well, she's done it often enough to Christine,' said my Mum, standing up for me and dragging me indoors at the same time.

Mum used to worry if no one was playing with me, and she bribed the boys with sweets to play round at our place. When the sweets were finished, the boys left. Once I dashed indoors, screaming my eyes out.

'They won't chase me, Mum. They won't chase me,' I cried. We had been playing kiss-chase and because I had two great candles dripping from my nose, nobody let me join in.

'Well blow your nose then,' Mum said, thrusting a bit of rag at me, 'And get along outside.'

I thought I had it over my Mum right from the start. When I used to wet myself I would tell her it was the cat.

'Oh no, Mum. That's the cat's fault. I didn't do it, Mum. Cat done that.' Or maybe I said it was the dog, if the cat wasn't around. One or other of the animals did most things, like forgetting where something was or throwing cabbage on the floor.

Mum was horrified at the first dirty joke I learned.

'There was this elephant in a circus called Nuts,' I told her. 'And someone shouted peanuts.' My Mum didn't get it immediately. 'So the elephant peed, Mum,' I shouted, and scarpered.

Dad was prone to pneumonia, and one year the river flooded and filled our home; Dad had a fit. He started frothing at the mouth and rushed around throwing and ripping the furniture. He ran out of the house and waded thigh deep through the flood water. Nearly all the local families had to be evacuated, but we were the last to be rescued and Dad was rushed into hospital with pneumonia.

He was back to his old self when he came out, and immediately set to teaching me how to drive and how to shoot.

'Take the car up the road,' he ordered. 'But if you hit anything, I'll hit you.' I never did hit anything, although my feet hardly reached the pedals, and I learnt to shoot better than him.

It was always Dad who gave me orders and told me how to help around the house. Mum just carried on waiting on me hand and foot, cooking and serving food, washing and ironing and making the bed. It was Dad whose word was law.

When I was nine, the school Health Inspector said that I was too skinny, and that I was suffering from malnutrition. He arranged for me to be sent to a holiday home in Littlehampton to be fattened up for a month. It was run by nuns, and when I arrived there were sixteen boys staying, but no girls. We were all as skinny as rakes. We bathed and played ping-pong and one of the older boys taught me how to play chess. It was the first time I ever felt myself aware of a boy.

It was not long before Dad made me my first bike, that Anne and I got into the papers for saving a man's life. We had been sliding on the ice that winter and when we slipped into the bushes by the garage for a pee, we found a man lying unconscious. We ran for help and the man was resuscitated. He had been suffocating from car fumes. When Mum heard about it, she was annoyed that the man never bothered to come and thank us.

As soon as I got my bike, I stopped seeing so much of Anne. She wasn't the tom-boy I was, and with my bike I was away with the boys after school. Throughout the summer we swung across the river on ropes, climbed trees and fought.

There was Tommy Jones with dark, short, curly hair. Keith, and Alan, the timid one, and Christopher, who was my age and always wanted to fight me. Christopher was the crazy one; he had been shell-shocked during the War and sometimes went off his head. He used to cut off the heads of birds.

Dad was brutal too. He drowned our dog's puppies. He put them all in a sack and shut me in my room, because I had asked for one to be saved and wouldn't stop whining about it. He just walked down to the river and dumped them in, keeping them under until they were dead. Once I brought a fieldmouse home. I held it out in my cupped hands, very pleased to have such a warm, living thing to play with. But Dad took it away from me. He threw it on the floor and crushed it under his foot. It squeaked.

When the school inspector came, I hid my bike in the fields because it didn't have any brakes – but it was a good bike. I started doing a paper round when I was twelve, and did it for two years on that bike. It meant getting up at six in the morning and riding six miles to fetch the papers, deliver them, and then get to school on time.

At school I learnt about the Scarlet Pimpernel and Sir Francis Drake. And I did mental arithmetic. I never got much credit for that, although it was my best subject. I used to get all the right answers, but the teacher insisted I use his algebraic method. Since I did it faster my way, I wouldn't, which made him cross. I just couldn't see the point. Looking back on it now, I think it was about that time that things started to go wrong in my life.

Nothing happens in a caravan without one being a part of it, even when you're supposed to be asleep. All the rows, all the decisions – you hear everything. And if you don't understand what's going on, you make up your own explanations for why people do such hurtful things to each other. But it doesn't stop you being hurt.

Around that time I was chosen by the school to throw the discus and javelin in competitions with other schools. But I just didn't want to. The trouble was that Mum and Dad didn't seem to care what happened to me at school. They didn't bother coming to Parents' Day and because they didn't care, I decided not to care whether I competed or not. Eventually the Headmaster himself called me into his study to try and force me to play against the other schools. I was far better than anyone else in our school, but I wouldn't be persuaded. He tried to reason with me, but nothing would change my mind.

Then my friend Anne moved into the class above me and made friends with another girl, which really upset me. I refused to talk to Anne. Once I passed her on my bike. She was walking with a boy and wearing a bit of lipstick. That was the end of our friendship, and I felt betrayed. She became ill soon afterwards, and died, which upset me even more.

'I don't believe in God any longer, Mum.'

The days when I had helped Dad take his car to bits, taken my bike apart and painted it, made go-carts and climbed trees, were over. We were changing. The boys were growing up. Because of my quickly-developing boobs I was nicknamed Sabrina, after a busty girl who was causing a sensation on TV just then, but I stayed in jeans longer than the other girls at school, who rushed into wearing skirts. Once, the man next-door-but-one asked me to hold his whatsit, and I did, because it was less risky to do it than not. He just pulled it out of his trousers and after I had held it for a moment, he gave me some money to buy sweets with. After that I avoided his house.

Whether it was because of that or because of Mum and Dad I don't know, but I now started feeling out of place. Everyone I knew seemed to fit in, to have a role. I was different, I felt awkward, as if I was beneath them all. Instead of passing off, the feeling grew, and I felt even lonelier.

Mrs Dreen up the lane had a granddaughter called Veronica Briggs who I was supposed to be accompanying to the cinema. I went round to Veronica's house wearing a skirt – it must have been one of the first occasions I had worn one – but all of a sudden Mrs Briggs decided that Veronica wasn't allowed to go, and wouldn't tell me why. I wouldn't leave until she did tell me: I knew there was a reason. When Mrs Briggs went to the lavatory, I locked her in and forced Veronica to tell me. They didn't think I was the right kind of friend for Veronica: I wasn't nice, I lived in a shabby railway-carriage. I suppose I had sensed it all along, but hearing it out loud like that tore at something within me.

I used to get fourteen bob a week for doing the paper round, and I topped up my wages by doing some babysitting. That lead to more trouble. If the fathers caught me alone in their houses, they often tried to kiss me. I didn't like it; their heavy bodies pressed against me sickeningly, and I was terrified that what I knew went on between men and women might happen to me. I just tried to get away from the brutes as quickly as I could, and wipe their foul saliva from my lips. My father presented the worst threat, because he was so close. It took me ages to get to sleep at night, and the only way I managed was to wedge my door shut with a shoe and keep a little knife under my pillow.

As soon as I was fifteen, Mum took me to the Employment Agency and they found be a job doing some typing in an office. After that, I had another five jobs, one after the other, and I hated them all.

'Well, if you're not happy at work, Christine, you come home,' my Mum said. So I stayed at home and did the cleaning, cooking and washing up, and she went to work instead. All this time, I wasn't speaking to Dad. I was terrified of him. I avoided and ignored him totally. This went on for over a year and eventually produced a rash of spots all over my body. Mum took me to the doctor who said it was a nervous disorder and sent me to a woman psychiatrist. It was Mum who cried in the consulting room.

'It's dreadful. I can't go on,' she told the psychiatrist. 'Christine won't speak to her father, and he won't speak to her.'

'Why not?' the psychiatrist asked me.

'I hate him. I hate him,' I cried. I couldn't say why, or explain it any more than that. All I knew was that I hated him.

'She'll have to go away from him until she calms down and sees reason,' the psychiatrist said.

So Mum and I went away to Redhill to stay with my uncle. Mum cried every day and spent every evening on the phone to Dad. She talked to my uncle, trying to sort things out, but after four days she couldn't take it any longer and went home, leaving me behind. I got a job in a tie factory, stencilling pictures of girls onto the ties. I only worked there a short while. The spots went, and I had to go home. My uncle and aunt had only just got married and didn't really want a fifteen-year-old girl in their house.

I still wouldn't speak to my father. I started staying out late at night to keep out of his way. I had met a nice boy named Peter.

'The door'll be locked at ten sharp. In or out,' he

26

warned. So I got locked out, and Mum cried and made a scene until he let me in.

She's a bad lot and there's no controlling her,' he told my Mum. 'She'll end up no good.'

I had to get out of the house, so it was back to the Employment Agency. The man there said he had found just the job for me. A dress shop in London wanted a model. Mum came up on the train with me to the interview. On the train a man called Tony Tenzer started talking with my mother. When he heard that I was going up to London for a modelling interview, he gave Mum his address.

'Do get in touch, won't you? I'm sure Christine is going to be a great success. She's very photogenic, you know.'

The interview went well and they gave me the job, which meant travelling to and from London daily. I met Tony Tenzer again on the train and he suggested I went to see a friend of his, Mark Henry, a photographer, to get some test shots done. It seemed like a good way of getting more work, so I went along to Mark's studio. I was quite frightened of him because he was queer and I had never met one before. The pictures we did of me wearing a bikini appeared in *Tit Bits*. Mum and Dad, as usual, didn't react at all. They were too wrapped up in their own problems to take any notice of me. So I just went off and did things on my own.

Somebody who did seem to care about me was the Ghana cleaner at the shop where I worked. He was always kind and smiled at me. I actually felt slightly superior to him, as I suppose one did in those days, which made a change from the way I felt in Wraysbury. One day he asked me whether I would come up to London at the weekend and help him with his studies. I didn't see why not. When I got there, he seemed less keen on his studies

27

and more keen on chatting to me. We talked quite a bit. I told him about myself and what life was like in the caravan. He told me how lonely he was in London, that he had no real friends.

'But it makes me so happy to have you here,' he added, leaning forward to kiss me. I let him, but when he wanted to move onto the bed, I panicked and got up to go.

'Don't worry, honey, we won't do it properly. We'll just play a bit, that can't do any harm. I'll show you.'

I was very curious. I had often wondered what it would be like, and since he had agreed not to go the whole way, I agreed and hopped on the bed. Of course once he started, he did go the whole way. I can't say I was stimulated by the experience, and once it had happened I wondered what all the fuss was about. I didn't feel as though I had lost anything very much at all. It didn't hit me until I was sitting in the train on the way home. Then I felt terribly ashamed of what I had done, and every time I thought about it I felt sick and unable to contain my dark, dreadful secret. I never saw him again.

The second time it was much better. My next man was an American soldier who was in digs with two other GI's not far from Wraysbury. I ended up staying the night with him quite often, and let him make love to me. It was warm and comfortable lying in his arms, and I was sorry when he had to go back to America. His wife, he told me, had been unfaithful to him and he was very upset. I was very upset to discover that he had left me pregnant.

I remember lying at home in bed at night, thinking it just couldn't be true.

Oh God, I prayed silently, it can't be true. Someone, please tell me it's not true. It can't have happened to me. What will they say? How can I get rid of it?

Castor oil, gin, whisky. Hot baths and steam 'til you

28

think you're passing into nothingness. All is black and your body floats above you, way above. Your body doesn't function. You feel weak and lifeless. But the life within you is still there, growing, beginning to show.

What will the neighbours think? They'll say what they think. They're the kind of neighbours who make sure they know exactly what's going on the whole time. You feel bad, you *are* bad. You've got yourself pregnant and the neighbours really will have something to talk about – unless you get rid of it.

Get rid of it. I can't do it. I have to. It's down there and it's got to, got to go. Push in a knitting needle. That's what they say works. Probing and poking with a needle until you know you've broken it. You must bear the agony 'til the pain makes you crazy. You can no longer think, 'Why?' You just poke and probe, knowing you'll die a worse death if you don't go on. So you do.

I felt it moving. It started pushing. No, not now. It's too soon. Nine months, they say, not six. It's supposed to be nine. Nine. Nine. Keep saying it, but don't cry aloud or they'll hear you. Perhaps the pain will kill me, but the pain goes, I can breathe. There's just a dull ache in my back. Then again it twists and pulls me apart. Everything inside me is falling out. They'll come and find me here, a mess on the bunk. Red. Red. Orange and yellow. The ceiling is yellow. The wooden plank splits across the ceiling. Don't scream. Don't cry out, they'll hear you. It'll go away soon now.

This is my Hell. Flames searing me, tearing at my flesh. Turning, twisting, tearing and surging through the whole of me. Breaking me. Tearing me. And then it went away, far away.

'Mum! Mum!' I cried when I saw its slimy, red mauve head. Half there. Not there and there again. She came.

29

Thank God. She came and saw the state of me and rode off on the bicycle to get the doctor.

My child was born. Naked withered and premature. A half-dead screaming infant leaving me with a gaping wound. They took him to hospital and he died. I couldn't sleep. There was no sleep for me. No peace. Just the pain, and then the shame.

3

LONDON

I COULDN'T stay at home any longer, so I decided to move to Slough with a girl friend from up the road, who had also got herself pregnant and was getting heavier by the week. We had both managed to save enough money to find lodgings, with a Polish man. We paid our rent and kept ourselves to ourselves whilst we looked around for jobs.

The Pole was very kind to us. He checked that we were all right, that the tiny cooker worked, wondered whether there was anything else we needed. It was fine for the first week, but then he started coming up to our flat too often. He could only have been about thirty, but he was fat and balding and, to us (then only sixteen), he seemed like an old man. He must have been lonely and he used to stare at us when we came in and went out. It could only have been about ten days after we moved in that he declared he loved me, and asked me to marry him.

'I can't marry you,' I said, 'I'm only sixteen, and I don't want to get married until I'm twenty at least.'

'But you can have everything a girl could possibly wish for,' he pleaded. 'This house would be yours, clothes, and many children.'

What? And then live happily ever after? I thought about it, but there was no way I could see myself actually going through with it. No, he definitely wasn't for me.

A little while after that, I came home one night and found him standing at the foot of the stairs, barring my way to the flat. I tried to get past him, but he grabbed my sleeve and pulled me into his kitchen, closing and locking the door behind us. I could smell the vodka as he pushed me against the wall and leered at me, heaving his hot body against mine. I screamed for Pat, as his ugly face loomed menacingly down again and his fat hands tore my dress from my shoulders.

Thank God Pat heard me. She rushed downstairs and started battering the kitchen door, shouting at him to open it. Luckily the Pole didn't want any of the other tenants to hear, and he let go of me to open the door. He tried to talk his drunken way out of the situation, but we just fled upstairs. We heard him go into the garden, where he lay moaning for a while.

We decided to move to London, where two fridge salesmen we had befriended told us there were rooms going in their boarding house. Why didn't we move there, they suggested, and when it got lonely we would have them for company? It seemed like a good idea; anyway there was nothing better, so we went.

We wandered round London looking for new jobs. I worked as a waitress in a Greek restaurant. It was hard work and badly paid. I got five pounds a week and my feet ached the whole time. They did give me an evening meal though, which helped, and if Pat came to meet me after work, which she sometimes did, they fed her too. It wasn't a bad place. The Greek owners were very jolly, and the customers were pretty friendly most of the time. It was difficult because Pat was getting very large and couldn't work any more, so I was trying to keep us both going.

Life wasn't exactly exciting. I was happy just to be able to get to sleep at night without worrying about everything that had happened. I had a boyfriend, a Greek boy, but I hardly went out because the money was so short, so I just dreamed that one day something would happen that would enable me to wipe out the past and completely change my life. I was lucky. That chance came, and when it did it seemed far more exciting than I had ever dreamed possible.

Chance came in the shape of a beautiful woman. She walked into the restaurant one night in a glamorous dress, her hair shimmering. She was amazing. All eyes turned as she walked past. The waiters, even the manager, scrambled to be courteous and friendly to her. I had never seen anything like her before. She came from another planet. The world of stardom, of impossibly glamorous magazine covers, where gorgeous, famous people drank wine, and women never had ladders in their stockings.

I couldn't take my eyes off her. She moved so gracefully, and laughed and talked so easily. She seemed to be and to possess everything a woman possibly could. When I went to clear her table, she actually talked to me. She asked if I was interested in trying for another job.

'Why don't you come and work at the Cabaret Club? That's where I work. The money's much better and it would be much more fun. Mr Murray, who owns the club is always looking for new talent and you've got just the right kind of looks.'

I was so excited.

'Me?'

'Yes, why not?' Well, why not indeed? But why? I couldn't believe what she was saying; it seemed too good to be true.

'I'll arrange for you to meet him,' she said, 'I know you'll do fine.'

'What do you have to do?'

'Dance on stage.'

It was unbelievable. What a brilliant opportunity! But I couldn't dance. I wouldn't be able to do it. Then I remembered I had been good at ballet until Mum had been unable to afford the classes any longer, so why not give the club a try?

I went along to the interview in a total state of nerves, but when I arrived the club was such a let down. It was really shabby. The faded red lamps stood on the tables and in the harsh light of day you could see the flaking paint and tarnished fittings. Where were the glittering costumes? Upstairs being patched by other girls? Where were the soft lights, the music, the romance? Where indeed? But eight pounds, ten shillings a week was a dream come true. It meant no more worrying about the rent or money for the gas meter. Maybe it was even a chance to become *someone* in this world.

'OK. Let's see if you can do anything.' Mr Murray motioned me to the stage. 'Put on a costume and just see if you can follow the routine.'

I had to follow the girl who had come to the restaurant. I was terrified and my heart pounded as I moved with the music. I just wanted to disappear before they threw me out.

'Right. Enough!' shouted Mr Murray. 'You're hired.'

I didn't believe it. It was fabulous! Fantastic and totally impossible. I wanted to run home and tell Pat, tell my Greek boyfriend and the fridge representatives. They'd never believe it.

I loved it when I first started work, really loved it. I began as an understudy and had to work with all the other girls to learn my steps. There were plenty of rules at the club. You weren't allowed to be late and you were fined if you were. You got fined for everything. For having laddered stockings or not wearing your silver shoes. You got the sack if you were discovered having anything to do with the waiters or customers.

It took a little while, but at last I felt that I belonged. Most of the customers were pampered old men, but we had a few parties with some of the Arab boys who came to the club. They were young, they laughed and had fun. After we finished work, they'd be waiting outside and take us out for a cup of coffee somewhere. Then we could relax and giggle and stop pretending to be nice to clients. The money quickly improved. The girl I had been understudying left, and once on stage I soon got the star part in the show. When we weren't on stage, we were allowed to sit out with the audience for a hostess fee of £5. That way I was soon making about thirty pounds a week. It was a real start in life.

4

MURRAY'S

ALTHOUGH MOST of the clients were old men – elderly and respectable business men, I mean – I did meet one or two younger people. One of these was a boy called Michael Lambton. He was a cousin of Lord Lambton's, and had been an officer in the Guards. I played hookey from the club sometimes and we went out for dinner or to the cinema. I don't think he really liked me working at Murray's, it wasn't quite the right place for an aspiring executive's girlfriend to work, and he often asked me to leave, but I took no notice.

Poor Michael. At one stage he was even banned from the club. It was New Year's Eve and we had been fooling around together. I ended up pouring a bottle of champagne over his head and he tipped the contents of the ice bucket over mine. It didn't go down well with the management. Nice ex-public school boys weren't supposed to do things like that, and they threw him out.

One night a rich Arab, Ahmed Kenu, who I had sat out with before, asked me to come and join him and his friends, a middle-aged man and a starlet, for a drink. As soon as I sat down the man, who was introduced as Stephen Ward, a fashionable osteopath and an artist, leant towards me.

'I saw you in the show. You were delightful. Will you dance with me now?'

I accepted, and while we danced he squeezed my arm. 'What are you doing later?'

'I'm going home,' I said, quickly pulling away.

'I'll take you home, if you like,' he suggested casually.

'Oh no, that's impossible. I really must go home alone.' I knew the tone of voice to adopt with this kind of man. They say they just want to take you home but that wasn't all they were after. Anyway, I had an evening lined up with my Greek boyfriend and I wasn't going to spoil it for an old man.

'Do men take you home sometimes?' he asked hopefully. 'You know I really must have your phone number.'

'Well . . .' I hesitated, thinking why on earth should I give it to you? – I'll never see you outside this place.

'Ah, Christine,' he murmured as I led him back to Ahmed's table, 'You are a very sweet person. I think you and I are going to be very good friends for a very long time.'

I didn't pay any attention to what he said but he continued chatting to me, ignoring his own date, which annoyed Ahmed. Sensing the ill feeling. Stephen stood up.

'I must have your 'phone number before I leave,' he insisted. Ahmed and I realised that he wasn't going to go until he'd got it.

'SW10256room5,' I gabbled, so he wouldn't catch it, but Stephen had a notebook and pen handy, and made me repeat the number until he'd got it. Then, wishing Ahmed a pleasant evening, he and his companion were gone.

So many men took my number without ever following it up that I was surprised when Stephen called the next day – not once but three times. I refused his invitations, but he kept on ringing and eventually I got used to the calls and even looked forward to them, for Stephen had great charm:

'I'm in my consulting-room, Christine, just waiting for my next patient, so I thought I'd see what you were up to . . .'

I kept putting off another meeting, though, until he found out where my parents lived; to put him off, I had told him that I was going to my Mum's for the weekend, and immediately he had to know where – and of course he knew Wraysbury, and even the street next to our little lane.

* * * * *

I saw his car pull up outside our cottage, watched him stroll up to the door and heard his knock. I opened the door.

'Hello – Christine!' He actually sounded surprised to see me. 'I was passing right by your door, so I thought I'd drop in – I've got a little cottage not far from here. Why don't you come and see it? I thought you'd enjoy the drive.'

'Well, I don't think I can,' I began and, since I could hardly close the door, I invited him in for a cup of tea.

Mum had never met any of my London friends, and she was surprised and pleased to see Stephen. He immediately dominated the room.

'I'm Stephen Ward. What a charming little place you have here. Absolutely charming.' He walked over to the window. 'And what a lovely view.'

'Yes, everyone likes it,' said Dad, who chatted to Stephen while Mum fussed around putting the kettle on and fishing cups out of the sink.

'We have a river running along the back.'

'But how absolutely marvellous,' laughed Stephen. 'My

38

cottage at Cliveden is beside the river too. I was hoping to take Christine to see it this afternoon.'

Whilst my father and Stephen went into the garden to admire the river I recovered from the shock of seeing Stephen and of hearing his voice, which I found the most attractive thing about him. My mother came up to me coyly. 'What a lovely man he is, Chris. Where did you meet him?'

'Oh, at the club. He's been ringing me every day – I can't get rid of him.'

'I think he's very nice.'

'Well, he wants to take me for a drive to his cottage.'

'Why don't you go?' She couldn't understand why I should refuse his invitation.

'Oh, I don't know.'

We were interrupted by Stephen, who came running up the back door steps laughing. 'I nearly fell in!'

During tea he told my Mum how wonderful he thought I was at the club.

'Well, you're a very lucky girl to have such a nice man take an interest in you, Chris,' said Mum as she glanced up at Stephen. 'I only wish I'd had the same when I was your age.'

Stephen pretended to be flattered. He knew that he had impressed my parents. 'London is a dreadful place, and for a girl with Christine's looks it can be even more difficult to survive. There are so many undesirable types trying to exploit girls.'

Mum and I immediately thought of white slave trading and discreet murders on Clapham Common.

'Yes, a dreadful, dreadful place,' Stephen laughed. 'Frightful, unless you know the kind of people who can help you.'

'Of course, you're quite right,' Mum agreed; 'That's just what Christine needs.'

'I don't know why you don't come for a drive, Christine,' he repeated for my Mum's benefit.

'Yes, why don't you?' said Mum, standing up. 'It's a lovely day for a drive. I wish I was your age, Chris, and had your opportunities.'

That settled it. We drove off, Stephen talking non-stop as usual.

'It's not very far. I've had the cottage some time. My friend Lord Astor let me have it about eight years ago – he's one of my patients, you know. Isn't it a simply marvellous day? I'm so glad you could come, Christine. I've been longing to show you my cottage and meet you again ever since I saw you dance – isn't that just simply marvellous?'

I laughed, caught up in Stephen's enthusiasm. Soon we reached Lord Astor's estate and drove through the park.

'Bill Astor is a very old friend,' Stephen explained, 'and Cliveden is still a power to be reckoned with. Famous people have always come here and still do – politicians, royalty, diplomats – and Bill entertains much as they did in the old days. The National Trust now manages the grounds. The costs are huge, you know; you need thousands of pounds to keep a place like this running.'

As he was talking I noticed a house ahead.

'That's not yours, is it?' It was enormous. I had imagined a tiny little cottage with roses climbing up the walls. This was a mansion by comparison. 'But it's huge!'

'Not really,' he said. 'Come inside and see for yourself.'

We walked into a magnificent reception room, which was quite empty. 'I never use this room,' Stephen explained. 'I really must get some furniture for it.' Although he was to repeat this constantly, the furniture never arrived.

The kitchen astounded me.

'Do you live here all the time?'

'Just at weekends when I can get away.'

'But there's so much food!'

'I don't believe in eating during the week but I always keep this place well stocked. You have to get away from London once in a while; if you don't, I think it drives you mad.' He pulled out his sketch pad. 'Sit down over there, I'll draw you.'

I was flattered, and kept as still as possible. As he drew he told me about his life. He had worked his passage to America and lived there on a shoestring until he had studied osteopathy, but he mainly told me about the people he knew. He was a terrible name-dropper. It slipped out that he had sketched most of the members of the Royal family. People like Prince Philip and Winston Churchill used to visit him. I was amazed that he knew all these people, let alone that they actually came to see him. I was terribly impressed by it all.

After a couple of hours Stephen drove me home and rushed off without stopping. I was so excited by the afternoon's events.

'Oh Mum! You should have seen the place. It's enormous. Honestly, imagine having a place like that just for weekends? He must be very rich.'

'Well I think you're a very lucky girl to have such a nice friend, Chris. You must keep hold of him.'

* * * * *

Stephen phoned me in London the very next day and asked if I would go out for a coffee. I said I was too busy, but he insisted and I felt I could hardly refuse.

'I'll meet you at three,' I said, although I hated the idea of putting on makeup that early in the day.

41

Stephen came to fetch me at three o'clock on the dot and we drove to the West End. He told me more about the famous people he knew and promised that I would soon be introduced to them. 'But Christine,' he insisted, 'I don't think the club is a very good place for you. You never have any free evenings.'

'But they're nice people. It's just like a school, really.'

'Why don't you try modelling instead? You'd have your evenings free then, and I think you'd be very successful. I could introduce you to someone who could help.'

'I tried it once in a small clothes shop. My mother approved, but I broke a full-length mirror, and scalded the boss's mother's foot.' Stephen roared with laughter.

'Did they give you the sack?'

'No, I left.'

'Well you could always try it again – properly this time.'

'Not in a place like that. The manager kept getting me into dark corners.'

'The dirty devil. Men are such bastards.'

'Only dirty old men,' I said, looking at him, wondering whether he was one. I decided he wasn't.

'So why did you leave home?' he asked very seriously.

'I didn't get on with my father.' I didn't want to elaborate. 'I'll have to get home soon, Stephen – I've got to get ready for work.'

'Oh, never mind. I tell you what, why don't I pick you up the same time tomorrow?' I wanted to put him off, as I had decided that I didn't want the relationship to go any further.

'You're a very beautiful girl, you know, Christine.'

'Well, I think you should 'phone me first,' I said, thinking that would give me time to think up an excuse, because I really didn't fancy him at all. He was far too old.

'Are you married?' I asked him. I thought if he was, it

was strange that the woman he had been with at Murray's hadn't been at the cottage. But if he wasn't, that was strange too.

'Good heavens, no! Marriage is certainly not for me,' he laughed.

As he drove me home he told me again, 'I like you very much, Christine,' and took another drag from the cigarette that constantly dangled from his lips. 'You're the first girl I've liked so much for a long time.'

'Thank you, but I must go,' I answered, reaching for the door.

'I'll 'phone you tomorrow then,' he called.

That night in the club I told Michael all about Stephen.

'No, I've never heard of him. Why? Is he a new boy-friend?'

I felt like teasing Michael. He was so easy to tease because it was so obvious that he'd do anything in the world for me, though of course I never let him do anything much – then.

'No, he's dreadfully old. I just wondered if you knew him. He seems to know everyone. He's quite important, a doctor to Lord Astor and other famous people. He draws portraits as well. He's quite famous, you know.'

Michael had never heard of him.

'I think he's quite lonely,' I teased, and told him about the visit to Stephen's cottage and the trip to the West End coffee bar that afternoon.

'Well, he sounds a bit of a crank to me.' I didn't take any notice because Michael was rude about people as a matter of course, although I knew he was soft underneath.

The 'phone rang the next morning. 'How about another drive?' It was Stephen as he had promised, and he was very insistent.

'I can't,' I pleaded. 'I've got to meet my boyfriend and then I've got to go to work.'

'Well, give it a miss,' he laughed. 'It's such a lovely day and a drive will do you good. You've got to have some life of your own, you know.' I thought about what he said. All this working at the club wasn't getting me anywhere. It was just a round of fat old men who came to watch the cabaret and then asked you sit out with them while they talked about dividends and market prices, and made the occasional corny remark. He was right, I needed some social life of my own. So I agreed to see him. At least he treated me like a human being, as an equal. He didn't look down on me, or leer like so many others.

We went to the same coffee bar, and sat chatting happily in the sun. Suddenly he shot out another of his crazy ideas.

'I wish you'd come and live with me. I've only got a small place but you're out from nine at night and I'm out all day, so we wouldn't get in each other's way at all.'

'I already have a room.' I wasn't going to have anything more to do him, he was far too old for me.

'But come and have a look at it anyway.' He sounded so offhand. I learned that he always did when proposing a scheme. He never put a lot of pressure on you, but his enthusiasm made you feel you were being silly and letting him down if you didn't accept. So once again I gave in and agreed.

We drove round to Orme Court in Bayswater, which wasn't a very good area then. His flat was tiny and on the top floor, although there was a lift. There was a bed-sitting room with two single beds pushed close together, and an adjoining bathroom. It was very clean and I liked it very much, especially the bathroom. I longed to have a bath in it.

We had had a bathroom in the caravan but no running water, and the bathroom at my lodgings was shared by all sorts of people, and always filthy. Compared to this flat the boarding house was dark and dirty and very depressing. There was no carpet on the stairs and the building smelled. You were lucky if your sheets were changed once a month and, worst of all, you couldn't sit on the lavatory because it was always wet. If the place still exists today I wouldn't be surprised to find the same foul conditions.

Stephen had put the kettle on for another cup of coffee. He drank at least eight cups a day.

'Caffeine's good for you,' he said, as I automatically reached for the cups. There we were, already a team.

I never felt any need for formality with Stephen, I just always felt relaxed with him. Soon I found myself telling him all about my life. He was a very sympathetic listener and quickly understood me. I told him about my life at home and a boy I had been particularly friendly with.

'He's the one you really like then?'

'Yes. He's called Peter. When I was pregnant he offered to marry me, but of course I couldn't because it wasn't his baby. Anyway my father didn't want me to. Nor did his. He was furious about our meeting because their family was much better off. Peter used to rub it in. He'd take me to the cinema then say he only did it as a favour!'

'Do you still see him?' Stephen was far more interested in Peter than the other boyfriends I'd told him about.

'Occasionally, when I go home for the weekend.'

Stephen and I were getting on really well.

'This is such a lovely little flat, and so neat.'

'It's just right, as I live alone and go to Cliveden at weekends. It's never been worth getting a larger place.'

We had some more coffee. I poured in the milk. 'How many sugars?'

'Two, baby, always two. I wish you would come and live here,' he said seriously. 'I feel that I've known you for

45

years. It would be so easy. I'm hardly ever here – you could call the place your own.'

It did sound nice, but I just wasn't sure of him. 'I'll think about it . . . I'm not very sexy, you know.'

'I don't want to make love to you, silly – I just like your company.' He sounded as though the whole idea of us having an affair was preposterous.

I thought about his suggestion a lot the next day. I also thought a lot about him. He was full of life, enthusiastic about everything. He never seemed to question what he was doing, just went ahead with it. He was always such fun and so charming. Someone who was never serious nor self-pitying, although he did talk a lot about other people and the impression they made on him, particularly the princes and princesses, dukes and duchesses, lords and ladies.

People loved him, too. He was marvellous company. Stephen would always fill an awkward silence with a funny remark, would never put you down for telling a flat joke. He wanted everyone to be as happy and carefree as he was, and was genuinely upset by a sad smile or drooping shoulders.

Of course he 'phoned the next day and we met for another cup of coffee. I was glad of his company, and I wanted his friendship. I felt that at last I wasn't alone in the world any more. Whatever happened there would always be Stephen. So I moved in.

As he had said, I hardly ever saw him. When I did it was late at night when I returned from the club. By the time I got up in the morning he had already left for his consulting room. After seeing his patients he would go straight away to meet a friend in a restaurant or coffee bar, armed with his sketch pad. He did a lot of sketching, and left a new drawing beside my bed each morning for me to look at when I awoke.

At the beginning he tried to discover whether I was interested in him sexually, but he never tried very hard. He always left me a way out, never forced me. Gradually we became like brother and sister. I used to come home at three or four in the morning to find Stephen reading. He never went to sleep until I was there beside him and had told him about my evening.

He was fascinated by the men I met. Did I fancy any of them, was I going out with anyone? He liked to share my feelings; I was his security. We didn't need any other companionship and I never bothered to make any close friends outside our own room.

One night when I got home Stephen was lying in bed and he told me all about this fight he had heard next door.

'You should have heard it, little baby; a prostitute and her ponce next door to this very room. You should have heard them arguing. He was hitting her and she was shouting, calling him names.'

'What did you do?' I wondered if he'd gone in to try and separate them.

'I can tell you it was first class entertainment, little baby. She started hitting him back. Listen! They've started again.'

I heard a girl yelling through the wall.

Stephen said 'Pass me that glass,' then he put it to the wall and listened through it.

'You can hear much better like this. She's screaming "You bastard, you bastard. Get out." She wants him to give her the money now. He's hit her again. Now she's hitting him, calling him a bastard, a thief and a pimp . . . Ooh, I think she must have hit him in the balls because he's groaning. He's threatened to come back later! What d'you think, little baby?'

Stephen was really excited. He laughed and laughed.

'And right next door to us. I thought this was a respectable neighbourhood. Fancy that sort of thing going on next door to us. We won't need the television any longer, will we, with action like that? Go to the window and see if you can see him going. I bet I know which girl it is. I see her come in in the evening, and she looks as if she's on the game.'

'Well, you should find out!' I laughed. Stephen's laughter was infectious.

* * * * *

Life at the club went on in an unchanging routine of work and fines. Sometimes the fines were so large I only picked up ten shillings of my regular wages at the end of the week. I was always being fined for being late and for not going for the statutory weekly visit to the hairdresser's. I also got fined for being bruised, and I bruise very easily. Bruises? They came in strange ways . . .

One night before I left for Murray's, Stephen insisted that I joined him for dinner with some friends.

'Oh baby, you must meet these people. Would you believe it, they like having sex with other people around. They think it's the ideal relationship for married couples. Oh come on. It'll be an experience for you.'

'What do they do?' I was very curious, it sounded so peculiar.

'They came to the cottage once and Bertie was having it off with one girl while Mary, his wife, had it off with another man,' Stephen laughed. 'All Bertie was interested in was whether Mary was enjoying herself! Really, little baby, doesn't it make you think – perhaps that's what it's really all about?'

48

Talking to Stephen made it sound as though it would be just a good laugh, so it seemed silly not to go. When we arrived at Bill and Mary's house we were already giggling with anticipation. I wondered what was going to happen – it was all getting too much for me. Then the door opened.

There were six of us altogether. Stephen and myself, our hosts Bill and Mary, and another couple, John and Carol. Everything appeared quite normal. It was a beautiful house with an elegant drawing-room and dining-room. The others were dressed up as though they were about to have their pictures taken for *The Tatler*. We sat down for dinner at the polished oak table piled with Georgian silver, and I suddenly realised that the ornament in the middle of the table was a huge plastic penis. It looked so peculiar; it just didn't go with the thick pile carpet and the lilies on the sideboard. I actually wondered whether they hadn't real-ised what it was, but I wasn't left wondering for long.

'Very attractive,' laughed Stephen, pointing at it. 'Where did you get it?'

'Germany,' said Bill.

'I suppose there's quite a demand for unusual ornaments there. They must turn them out by the thousand. How's that for a laugh, little baby?' I giggled with embar-rassment.

'A friend showed them to us,' explained Bertie, and Mary added: 'They've got them in all sorts of shapes and sizes. And some of them are hairy.'

'Ooh!' squealed Stephen.

'And one had dragon's spines. We were simply terrified coming through customs!'

'What on earth would you say if they caught you with that in your case?' wondered Stephen.

'Mine was shot off in the war. Be a good chap, that's for my wife's convenience,' chortled Bertie. 'They're jolly useful, aren't they? You use them on different girls all the time, don't you darling?'

'Pass the salt, please,' said Stephen quickly. 'Mmm, wonderful dinner. I love curries. What do you think, Christine?'

'Wonderful,' I lied, fighting to swallow the stuff.

'What's it made of?' asked Stephen, back to the penis again.

'A kind of plastic.'

'Just look at the size of it, Christine!' I wasn't quite sure where to look or what to do, so I smiled and decided this must be how people in grand houses always behaved.

'Christine is a very dear little girl,' Stephen said. 'She works in Murray's Cabaret Club.'

'And I've got to be there at nine-thirty.'

'Well in that case, my dear, we'll finish dinner a little earlier than usual,' said Mary cheerfully, giving me a condescending smile.

When everyone had finished eating, Mary disappeared. She returned a few minutes later dressed in a straw skirt with about ten straws hanging from it. What do you do? Laugh? Look the other way? Or do what everyone else does? The others started taking their clothes off, and Stephen helped Bertie open the sofa into an enormous bed. Soon I was the only one with any clothes left on. Even Stephen was taking his trousers off. It occurred to me that all the the men must have been forty at least, but us three girls were fairly young. I didn't feel at all sexy. Sex to me was something you did with one other person, quietly and in the dark.

Stephen came up to me. 'Off with your clothes,' he laughed. Well, what could I do? I took them off. Bertie was already on top of Carol, and Stephen was laughing as he watched them. Then Bertie caught one of my breasts

50

and started playing with it. I moved away. It seemed so extraordinary that someone could actually be having it off with one person and playing with my tits at the same time. Was this good clean fun? Well, it was different. But it definitely wasn't sexy.

Bertie had finished with Carol, and came towards me. 'Oh no you don't,' I thought, 'I certainly won't let you put it inside me'. He didn't insist, he just went down on me, which I must admit I enjoyed so much that I let him put it in. I came. Then I had had enough. Stephen meanwhile just stood by watching, laughing at the whole thing. Then our hostess came over and started going down on me. I just let it all happen. Stephen eventually joined in, as Mary jumped up to fetch a whip from the coffee table which she handed to him.

'You naughty little baby,' laughed Stephen, looking down at me with Mary still at it, and he brought the whip down on my stomach. That was enough. I was going. That bloody hurt.

I pulled on my clothes.

'Sorry, little baby.'

'Oh, that's OK.' The others were carrying on regardless. 'I've got to go to the club now.'

'Christine's got to go,' announced Stephen.

The others looked up for a moment. 'See you again soon, I hope.' They were so casual about it, so offhand. A few more parties like that and I was convinced that titled people, rich ones with Bentleys and country estates, lived like that as a matter of course.

Stephen saw me to the door and stood there, quite naked, for the world to see. 'Don't be annoyed, little baby,' he grinned. 'I'll see you later.'

Back at the flat later on, I told him that I didn't really like orgies.

'You're too self-conscious. You shouldn't think about it so much. Bodies are only bodies. We all have them.'

'I know, but I still don't like orgies.'

'Well, nor do I,' agreed Stephen. 'Except that they're quite amusing to watch, although I never seem to get a hard-on.' Stephen must have been a little worried that he had upset me, because he said. 'You still want to live with me, don't you?'

'Of course I do,' I said truthfully. I couldn't imagine living with anyone else now.

'I think I can afford to move into a larger flat, you know, and after working so hard for so many years I think I deserve a reward.'

'But it's lovely here.'

'But if we got a house we could entertain.'

'Not orgies?'

'No – bridge parties, invite a few friends. We could even get married.' He put his arm affectionately around my shoulders. 'You know I love living with you. I couldn't stand sharing with another man. They're messy and hateful. And they're so lazy, they leave their clothes lying all over the place.' He hated untidiness, and liked having me around because I made few demands.

'We'd have the ideal marriage. Both of us could do just as we pleased, without jealousies or questions, yet we would always have each other.'

I had my doubts but didn't say anything. I knew Stephen well enough to know that he wouldn't push it; he would let me decide. But he was determined about moving.

'We'll look for a house tomorrow. I know just the person to ask: Peter Rachman. He's an estate agent, and a very good friend of mine. He'll find us a really nice place with plenty of space. You can even have your own little room if you like, and I'll be next door if you need me.'

52

5

PETER

PETER RACHMAN was a strange person. Like Stephen he laughed a lot, but it was a pretence, for his eyes never lost their cold, glittering hardness. He was a Polish refugee who had arrived in Britain at the end of the War. With a steel-hard nose for business, he bought up a vast number of houses in the slum areas of London and then let them to black families who were prepared to pay his high rents because no-one else in those days would consider them as tenants. Most landlords didn't want to 'dirty' their lodgings with even one black family. As soon as one family moved in, their cousins and friends would follow. And then the white families would give notice, which, of course wouldn't do.

Not that Peter was acting philanthropically. He just knew a good business prospect when he saw it. Peter was unswervingly strict about rent arrears. Black was black and white was white, and if you didn't pay the rent, it was your look-out. 'You agreed on ten pounds a week for the room' he would say, 'and it's your business to see that the money is paid. I have to pay the overheads.' Just in case there was trouble – and sometimes there was – Peter took with him an armed guard and a pack of alsatians.

A few years after I met Peter, the methods he used to extort rent from his tenants were exposed, and I discovered just how foul they were. Peter never seemed to really understand what the fuss was about, or else he had perfected the mask of innocence. It seemed to those of us who knew him that he thought he was just getting what was owed to him. That might include all kinds of methods of eviction, like locking tenants out at night, or taking their furniture away. But sometimes if they didn't leave, he terrorised them with dogs and guns. To good tenants he was lenient and he was extremely generous to his friends. If you were white, intelligent and Peter liked you, he might let you live free.

Stephen and I visited Peter in a mews flat in Bryanston Place where he introduced us to a girl called Sherry who was living there. I sat and listened while Stephen and Peter talked about finding us somewhere to live.

'There's no problem about a place; I can find you a nice little flat, Stephen. That's fine. And what about some dinner, can you both join us tonight?'

Stephen was delighted with the invitation. If there was one thing he really liked it was being taken out to dinner. He was far too mean to take anybody out himself, although he did feed his friends at Cliveden. He was actually a very good cook, and quite houseproud. He was always terribly tidy and fastidious about personal appearance. His fingernails were always spotless and he cleaned the wash-basin after him – little things like that, although he didn't actually bathe very often.

At the restaurant, Sherry followed me into the Ladies.

'You must come and have tea tomorrow, Christine, so we can have a good chat.'

I accepted gladly. Sherry was very beautiful. She had great poise and she wore false eyelashes, things I had never seen before and immediately started wearing. It wasn't until much later that I found out that Peter had got her to arrange the whole meeting so that he could see me again.

When I went round to Bryanston Mews, Sherry and I had a good time chatting and talking about makeup. She showed me how to put on the eyelashes and how to do my face so that you would never guess I was wearing makeup.

Sherry was fascinated by Stephen.

'What's it like living with him?'

'It works very well. How long have you lived here?'

'Well I don't *live* with Peter you know, although it is his house. I'm Raymond's girl friend. Have you met him yet?'

'No.'

'His full name is Raymond Nash and he has a lot to do with financing gambling clubs. But he's married, you know, so we don't see each other very often.'

It didn't sound like a very happy relationship.

The afternoon went as Peter had planned. He turned up, as if by chance though of course Sherry had been expecting him, and when we had chatted for a bit, he suggested a game of chess. Half-way through the game he looked at me through narrowed eyes.

'I don't think I could trust you, you're too shrewd a chess player.'

It was a strange thing to say, but I didn't think much about it. I was enjoying myself. Sherry was great fun to be with, and it was nice to see someone new. Someone apart from Stephen, or the girls at Murray's. All too soon it was seven o'clock and I had to think about going home and getting ready for work.

'Go?' Peter arched his eyebrows. 'What for? You must stay and we'll all go out for dinner, somewhere really good.'

'Oh yes, you must stay,' insisted Sherry, who always agreed with Peter.

'But I've got to go to work.'

'Work? At this hour?'

'I work at the Cabaret Club.'

'But I thought you lived with Stephen?'

'Yes I do, but I still have to go to work, don't I?'

Peter was genuinely shocked.

'I don't understand. Do you mean to tell me that you live with Stephen and he doesn't even keep you? I've heard he's mean, but he can't be that mean.'

'It's not like that. He doesn't have anything to do with me – not in that way – I mean I don't go to bed with him or anything.'

'What!' Peter was appalled. 'I don't believe you. What do you mean by living with a man who isn't even paying you – and working in a club? I really don't think it sounds like a good idea at all. You should be living with a girl in that case. Anyhow, working in a club will soon wear you out – in a few years time you'll have nothing to show for it but a lined face. Why don't you do a little modelling? Sherry does some – she could help you – and there's plenty of room for you here.'

'Yes,' Sherry added quickly, 'I'd love to have you here. Raymond's away so much of the time – I'd just love it if you came to stay. It would be much more fun.'

It sounded quite logical. I began to wonder what I was doing wasting my life living with a much older man, and I liked the idea of moving in as soon as Peter suggested it; I would have agreed to move in with Sherry even without their urging.

'Give up the club,' Peter ordered. Peter made the decisions. He always took the responsibility for other peoples' lives.

'Give up the club and I'll lend you a few bob until you get started with the modelling. You can move in here straight away.'

I was too much of a coward to tell Stephen what I was

going to do, so I just left without saying anything. At first I liked the life in Bryanston Mews, and giving up the club was a dream. But I couldn't have chosen to live with anyone more different from Stephen.

Stephen was an artist who found beauty in the mind as well as the face. But Peter was entirely materialistic. As far as he was concerned beautiful girls were no more than chattels. Their only function was to make themselves more desirable. He loved buying me clothes to wear and would think nothing of giving me a luxurious fur or evening dress which he could then admire me in. Sometimes he would bring me jewellery, silver bangles and wonderful gold earrings. Or he would give me money to spend on something lovely – as long as I looked good. He paid for the most expensive makeup, a new scent, and for all my hairdo's, which was brilliant. He delighted in taking Sherry and me out, one on each arm, and swinging into his restaurants (he wouldn't eat anywhere else in case he was poisoned). Or he took us both out for a spin in the Cadillac, so that he could revel in the envy of other men.

I soon came to rely on Peter's 'few bob' and so I effectively became another bit of his property. And when Peter bought a woman, he made quite certain the whole world knew whose property she was. He also made sure I knew which side my bread was buttered. I could take all the gifts and cash I wanted, but in turn I was expected to be prepared for his visits to the flat.

Stephen was livid when he found out. I overheard him swearing at Peter down the phone, then he'd ring me and try and persuade me to meet him for a coffee. Eventually I agreed to see him, as long as Sherry was there too.

Stephen was to the point:

'You're doing the wrong thing, Christine. It never pays to get things the easy way, you know.'

I shrugged.

'But I like him, Stephen, honestly I do. I wouldn't do it if I didn't.'

'Like him or his money? I'll tell you, Christine, you're being a very silly girl. What kind of reputation do you think you'll earn living with a man like Peter Rachman? Being seen as his plaything? Don't expect that you're anything else, that there haven't been girls before and won't be girls after you.'

But it didn't make any difference. Peter had told me that Stephen was just a silly, bitchy old woman, eaten up with jealousy. By going on at me, Stephen only confirmed what Peter said. Living with Peter, you soon learnt he was always right. I soon stopped thinking for myself. If I ever had any doubts, it didn't take him long to make me see things the way he did.

Peter's way of life seemed absolutely all right to me. It was luxurious, it wasn't encumbered with worries; and he always gave me as much cash as I needed. Peter usually carried a fat roll of two or three hundred pounds with him, and paid cash as a matter of course.

Sex to Peter Rachman was like cleaning his teeth, and I was the toothpaste. It wasn't pleasant – it wasn't unpleasant. He always came round in the afternoons. I don't doubt there was another girl set up somewhere for the mornings and probably another for the night, unless he went home to his wife. He certainly never stayed the night with me. But in the afternoon he'd arrive, and without ceremony, take me roughly by the arm and push me in front of him into the bedroom.

He was a small, fat and bald man. He always made me sit on top of him facing the other way so I never saw his face. Although Peter was jealous of his possessions, his lovemaking was cold and clinical. He didn't believe that a girl could have a platonic relationship with a man.

'If I ever catch you fucking any other man I'll chuck you out,' he warned, but it never entered my head that he would, nor that if he found me alone with a man he'd immediately assume that we'd had sex.

Peter had never really got over being in a Russian concentration camp. He told me that it was during his imprisonment that he had vowed to himself that one day, at whatever cost in human misery, he would be rich enough to buy the flash American car that had driven past the miserable file of prisoners behind the barbed wire.

He had suffered enough. Too much to ever feel any sympathy for anyone else. His suffering scarred him; he no longer trusted anyone. If you offered him a glass of water, he'd go to the kitchen and thoroughly wash the glass before refilling it and drinking. Years after his escape he still hoarded crusts of bread under his bed. No one dared touch them, they were his security against starvation. Meanwhile, he happily ate the fillet steaks at one of his restaurants.

Peter was very proud of me.

'Leave your false tooth out,' he ordered in his high pitched Polish squeak, 'it makes you look cheeky.'

Rather than lose me, he bought me a sports car so I could visit my parents at the weekend. Dad, as I said, had taught me to drive when I was just a kid, so I didn't bother with lessons or a licence. Sometimes Peter came too, just for an afternoon. My mother liked his down-to-earth attitude to life. As soon as Peter had left, I'd race off in the car. I was a bit bored without boyfriends of my own age, but the car made up for that, although Peter didn't like me disappearing in the car. He was convinced I was seeing someone on the sly, and predictably enough he put his boys onto me.

One night I was driving through London. It was late but

I'd just gone out for a breath of fresh air, when a heavy Vauxhall cut across and waved me down. I guessed it was Peter's boys but there was nothing I could do. I made sure the locks were fast and sat in the car and waited. I watched the thug come towards me and wound down the window just enough to hear what he said. He was a large man and he told me Peter didn't like me going out late at night.

'You'd better get straight back to the flat, Mr Rachman's waiting.'

I was terrified, I just didn't want him to turn nasty.

'All right,' I said to get rid of him. He stared at me. I couldn't tell whether he was going to do anything. At last he turned and walked slowly back to the Vauxhall. I gave a huge sigh of relief. It could have been much worse. Peter was a dangerous man when things didn't please him and I knew I was lucky to get off as lightly as I did.

That wasn't the end of it. I was getting fed up with Peter's world and began spending more time with my parents. I would go away for the whole weekend. The crunch came when I got in touch with the other Peter, my old boyfriend. When I got back to London I told Rachman that I'd spent the whole time with my parents, helping about the house. He didn't believe a word of it. He often lost his temper and would take a swipe at my face or punch whatever came to hand – the wall, the bed – anything. Then he'd laugh it off, 'You little bastard!'

I didn't care. He wasn't going to make me do what he wanted anymore. I had my own life to lead. I decided I would go to Wraysbury for a week. This time Peter didn't fool around. He decided to bring me to hand and drove down with one of his boys to do just that. We, my Mum, Dad and I, were sitting having tea when he burst in.

'Give me the car keys!' he shouted at me in front of everyone. There was obviously no point arguing.

'And if you decide to come back, see to it that you behave yourself!' Grabbing the keys he stormed out.

I decided I wasn't going back. I had had enough of being owned. During our six months together I had grown to respect and even to like Peter Rachman for what he was: unscrupulous maybe, definitely a law unto himself, but a man who at least lived according to his *own* ideals.

6

MANDY

DURING MY affair with Peter Rachman, Stephen had
moved into Wimpole Mews. When I told him I had left
Peter, Stephen was delighted to have me back and genuinely forgave me for having been so stupid.

It was as though I had never gone, just the two of us
again.

'Just like we planned, little baby. You've got a room of
your own.'

It was tremendous to get into the swing of my own life
again. Despite several angry letters from Percy Murray
accusing me of breaking my contract with the club by
running off without notice, I soon talked him into giving
me my job back. I had a lot of time to myself as Stephen
had made a new friend, a Russian, Eugene Ivanov, the
new naval attaché at the Russian Embassy. I usually saw
Stephen for coffee in the afternoon. We'd have a good
natter then he'd be off socialising with Eugene. At the
weekend we often went to Cliveden.

I saw Michael Lambton again at the club. He was as
mad as ever about me, wanting me to give it all up to go
and live with him. But I was really enjoying my life now. It
was too much fun to give up for a man I didn't love.

The young Arab boys still came to the club and they
organised some wild parties after the club had shut for the
night. Several new girls had joined the cabaret, one of

whom I noticed in particular. She came from Birmingham, was about fifteen and very tarty. She piled on the foundation, using far too much powder. Worst of all, her eyes were coated with bright green eye-shadow. Having been shown by Sherry how to apply makeup discreetly, I really looked down my nose at Mandy Rice-Davies.

Mandy was popular with the Arab boys, and so despite my efforts to steer clear of her, it always ended up with us both being invited to their parties. The parties were good, and eventually we were both going out with Arab boys, who shared a flat. Although Mandy and I had our own rooms, she had a poky room in a boarding-house somewhere, and it was much more fun staying at the boys' flat. It meant that we both had company during the day and someone to travel to work with at night.

Living together, we inevitably became friends. Since I was slightly older and knew the club, I tended to be the leader. I showed Mandy how to do her face properly and gave her a lot of the expensive clothes Peter had bought me. I enjoyed having a friend to giggle with. It made a change from Sherry, who was always moaning about something; she was the kind of person who is determined to have a bad time. Although she hardly ever saw Raymond, rather than get out and enjoy herself, she preferred to mope and make a martyr out of herself.

My life was changing. It seemed like an age since I had left Peter and now I stopped going home to see my parents so often. I was independent, my own person and I much preferred seeing my own friends. I felt it was about time to get my own flat.

One afternoon I was in the bath, and Mandy was on the loo chatting to me. She was fed up because she thought she would have met all sorts of exciting people at the club by now, and had imagined that she was going to be carried away by a rich, handsome prince to live happily ever after. But it hadn't happened like that.

Men never took Mandy very seriously. They couldn't, because she was such a birdbrain – except where money was concerned. I was always the one boys were serious about and, typically, I didn't want that kind of relationship. Mandy, on the other hand, could never keep a boyfriend for more than a week. She was too shallow.

Anyway, we decided that we were fed up with work and fed up with Arabs. We felt underpaid and overtired.

'Let's leave the club,' I suggested, 'and get a flat together. It's worth a try. Even if it doesn't work out, we can always go back to Murray's. He's taken me back once, he'd do it again.'

'But what would we do instead?' Mandy was much more shrewd. She worried about where her cash was coming from, even before she needed to spend it. I never did. It always came, somehow.

'Well, we can model. And there's always Michael.'

'What, Michael from the club. The tall, handsome one?'

'Yes. He's always going on at me about working there. He'd love it if we got a flat together. I could tell him he could see me every night and he'd pay for the flat.'

Mandy seemed doubtful.

'Don't you believe me?'

'Of course I do.' Mandy was a bit in awe of me.

'Well, what are we waiting for? Let's get our own place. We'll find somewhere brilliant. And go out in the evenings . . .'

'With whoever we want . . .'

'One day's modelling will get us as much money as we earn in a week at the club.'

'We'll give parties . . .'

'It'll be great.'

I 'phoned Michael, who was delighted.

'Of course, I'll be able to see you every night,' I said. 'Isn't it a wonderful idea? We can do some modelling, but you'll have to lend us some money for the rent, until we can get everything sorted out.'

Michael agreed to lend us fifty pounds. So we looked for a flat and found one in Comeragh Road in West Kensington. I left Stephen again without any explanation. No conversation, no note, nothing. Mandy owed her landlady a month's rent, so we decided to move her and her things out in the middle of the night.

Mandy had a lot of stuff, so I rang Michael at midnight and asked if he could bring his car round to help.

'Can you park round the corner?' I asked him. We didn't want the landlady's attention alerted by the slightest thing.

He was suspicious immediately.

'What are you up to? It's a funny time to move, isn't it?'

'Nothing, Michael, honestly. Please come round.'

'But why on earth do you want to move now? It's the middle of the night.'

'We just want to move to Comeragh Road as soon as possible.'

Michael sighed, but agreed to help. We looked out for him and when we saw the car, we crept downstairs, our arms full of clothes. Naturally, the stairs creaked. Then Mandy had to drop a teddy bear, which bumped all the way down. The landlady's door opened and she rushed out to see what all the noise was.

'And what do you think you are doing at this time of night, Miss Davies?'

The minute I saw her, I ran out of the house to the car and leapt into the seat.

Michael and I waited for ages, but Mandy didn't appear.

'Go and see what's happened,' I ordered Michael.

'It's nothing to do with me.'

He was acting annoyed with me that I'd involved him in the moonlight escape. Secretly he was enjoying every minute of it.

'Well, I'm not going in.'

We waited another half-hour, then I decided to go and ring her.

Mandy was in tears. 'She won't let me go. She's threatened to call the police if I don't pay.'

'Don't worry, we'll sort something out,' I assured her and returned to the car. I told Michael what had happened and he laid out another forty pounds.

*   *   *   *   *

Comeragh Road was wonderful. It was the first place I'd ever had, and I was really proud of my flat. We had some great times there. I was determined to make up for all the evenings I had lost working at the club. One evening we put on our best dresses and went to an expensive restaurant. We ordered champagne and acted like duchesses. Everyone wondered who we were. The bill came to thirteen pounds – a lot in those days – so Mandy grabbed the sweet trolley on the way out, to make sure we got our money's worth, and escaped into a passing cab. It was wonderful to imagine the looks on the faces of the other customers if they had seen our legs dangling out of the cab window, whilst we stuffed our faces with sweets, giggling madly on champagne.

When we got back to Comeragh Road, we rushed into the landlord's flat and threw ourselves onto his bed, not realising he was there with his girlfriend. Luckily, they just laughed at us.

The next morning we were broke and still had no jobs, so we devised a wonderful plan to fool Michael. Mandy rang Michael to tell him to come round quickly. I was ill. I hadn't actually seen him once since moving in, so I wasn't greatly in favour, but he was our only hope.

'You must come round, Michael,' Mandy said pathetically, 'Christine's very ill.'

'What's wrong with her?'

'Well, the doctor came, and he said she'll have to have an operation. Just please come round, Michael, she's been asking for you. But you won't be able to stay long,' she added, remembering that we had invited our two Persian boyfriends round later, 'because the doctor says she's supposed to rest.'

I covered my face with white powder and waited in bed for Michael. I don't think he believed I was as ill as I made out, and when I asked him if he could lend me seventy pounds for the operation he adamantly refused.

'I've given you quite enough money already,' he snapped, 'and I can't carry on just handing it out like this.'

'But, Michael,' I moaned weakly, and Mandy added, 'It's time for your medicine, Christine.' Very convincingly she poured out a spoonful of diluted strawberry jam. I pretended to choke on the bitter taste.

'Oh, please, Michael,' I pleaded. 'You're the only person in the world who will help me. I promise, the minute I'm better, we'll go out together.'

Eventually he was forced to submit, and in the nick of time because Mandy and I only just managed to get rid of him and get ready before our boyfriends turned up. Poor Michael, I really had him on a string, but I was far too young ever to be able to take him seriously.

But that got us over the immediate crisis, and of course I spent so much time with the Persian boyfriend, whom I had become very fond of, that I hardly saw anything of Michael. I didn't see anyone else either, really, until my boyfriend went off to Persia for a few weeks' holiday. Then I rang Stephen, for the first time since I had left.

'Where on earth are you, you naughty little baby? I've been worrying about you, leaving like that without a word.'

'Oh, Stephen!' It was good to hear his voice again, 'You must come round. I'm living in Comeragh Road with a girl called Mandy. You must meet her. I'm sure you'd like her.'

Stephen came round to see us quite often and introduced me to his cousin, a former pilot in the Battle of Britain. He soon developed a terrible crush on me and for a while I really thought I loved him. He was terribly romantic, and loved holding hands. To me he seemed the perfect gallant hero, although far too old for me. We used to go out as a foursome with Stephen and Mandy and it wasn't long before the pilot had a key to the flat and was practically living with me.

One day he told me that his divorce was finally through. He was terribly excited and planned to move in with me properly. Everything was arranged, but when the day came, I got cold feet. I'd completely changed my mind and with Mandy's help composed a note telling him so, also asking if he could leave the key behind. When we heard him coming, we left the note out on the hall table and hid under the bed in the next room. We could hardly stop giggling out loud. Poor man, he left without a word, leaving his key behind.

When Stephen heard he really was cross at first. Then, as usual, he forgave me.

'You naughty little baby. You hurt him terribly.'

'Well, he should have known that I couldn't possibly

have lived with him, not really. What did he have to offer? I'm sure it's only his pride that's hurt. Anyway, I just couldn't go through with it, Stephen.'

'You're right, little baby. He'll get over it.'

The evenings were considerably emptier after the pilot had left, and we were stuck for things to do when our Persians were busy. One evening Nina Gadd, a friend of Mandy's, rang and asked us for dinner with some men, purely on a sex-for-money arrangement. At first we weren't sure whether to accept. It depended whether the Persian boyfriends were coming round. But hunger and the lack of money won, and we accepted.

Neither Mandy nor I had had much success modelling, probably because we hadn't taken it seriously enough. So we were grateful for what money we could get, to pay for food and rent. We went to quite a few of Nina's dinner parties and one evening at the Dorchester, we bumped into Peter Rachman. He was still rather fed up with me, but he was delighted by Mandy. She was just the type of girl he needed. A pretty face, and happy to be just that and no more. He took her out several times, but refused to come to Comeragh Road because I was there.

Whilst Mandy had met Peter, I had been introduced to Major James Eylan, who was very keen on going to bed with me. He was quite handsome but our relationship, though it lasted two years, was based purely on money. Although he always took me out to dinner or to a show and certainly knew how to give a girl a good time, I always expected him to leave me some money.

Stephen's affair with Mandy had deteriorated quickly.

'She's just a mercenary girl. Not a grain of sensitivity in her body,' he told me.

I first met Lord Astor at Comeragh Road. Stephen brought him round to spend the evening with Mandy and me, and we spent a very jolly time with Bill running after one or other of us, trying to pinch our bottoms. We giggled until our sides ached, drank quite a bit and sat around telling funny stories. Stephen had known Bill since the beginning of the 'Fifties when he had come to be treated after a hunting accident. They became close friends and Stephen was always welcome at the family seat, Cliveden.

When Mandy and I next found ourselves stuck for the rent money, Stephen produced a cheque made out by Bill. Presumably, this was an investment in future pleasures. The cheque was welcome, but Mandy and I had decided to pull up our roots. We were off to seek our fortunes in France!

It was a fairly hairy trip. We pinched a car and drove to the South of France. Got broke, dumped the car and got money from men. We dined at the best hotels and hitch-hiked in high heels and hats. God knows what we *didn't* get up to that holiday.

We returned to London to find we had lost our flat. Mandy moved in with Nina Gadd, and I moved in with my Persian boyfriend, which was a bit awkward as the lodgings were for male students only. The Persian was quite a bit different: he had a distinctly sadistic streak in him, and I must admit I quite enjoyed it when he threatened to hit me for disobeying him, although I cried when he did.

During the day he used to study and in the evenings he went out with different girls. I just couldn't accept that he should treat girls the same way I treated men – perhaps that was why I was attracted to him.

'I'm going out tonight,' he would announce, as he left me in the morning.

'Oh, please don't. I want you to be with me,' I used to plead.

70

'I'll see you later,' he snapped.

That meant two o'clock in the morning, drunk. I hated waiting up for him, but refused to go to bed before he got home. Sometimes I used to chase round the West End looking for him in the clubs. But if I eventually found him, laughing and talking with his friends, he just ignored me.

I took it all because I was crazy about him, but it really hurt. I would get quite desperate and clutch at his sleeve and make a terrible scene. Anything to get my own way, but he only enjoyed me when he had me pleading and cringing. He used to keep a whip on top of the wardrobe as a constant threat. Needless to say, the relationship didn't last long, but it was he who ended. it.

One day he just told me to get out. I couldn't understand it; I had done everything for him and yet he didn't want me. The classic story. Other men, who I didn't care for a bit, would have given me the world. In desperation, I telephoned Stephen again.

'Come straight round, little baby. Everything will be all right, darling,' he promised.

This time I thought I would stay with Stephen forever, I went round to Stephen's and later he drove me back to collect my clothes. When we got to the lodgings, Stephen waited for me in the car. Upstairs I found the Persian sitting on the bed, showing his photographs to another girl. I screamed and rushed at him, furiously hitting him, then ran out to the car with all my clothes.

'This time I'm staying,' I promised Stephen. 'Come on, let's go home and watch TV, Panorama's on.' It seemed like the end of a nightmare, but I didn't know what was waiting round the corner.

7

STEPHEN

STEPHEN WAS still very friendly with the bear-like Russian called Eugene Ivanov. Captain Ivanov had come to England in 1960 as an Assistant Naval Attaché at the Russian Embassy. Huggable as he looked, Eugene approved of me no more than he did any of Stephen's friends. I seldom saw him, as he and Stephen used to spend time playing bridge at Stephen's club, the Connaught, or in the coffee bar.

On the rare occasions when Eugene came to the flat, he normally had a cup of coffee whilst waiting for Stephen to get ready. Stephen was invariably late. As far as Eugene was concerned, I didn't exist. He didn't exactly disapprove of me openly, but he kept his distance. He seemed to me the kind of person who took pleasure out of other peoples' activities, rather than participating himself. A slight frown showed disapproval. A wry smile appeared on his face when he was amused by the conversation.

It was because of Eugene that Stephen met a little man in a black bowler hat in the restaurant up the road. It was early in June.

'You'll never guess, little baby,' Stephen said, 'But I'm going to meet a cloak and dagger man in a few minutes.' And he disappeared for dinner.

The cloak and dagger man, who called himself 'Mr Woods' (his real name, I learned long afterwards, was

Keith Wagstaffe), came back with Stephen, and I made coffee for them while he asked Stephen a lot of questions about his relationship with Eugene. He didn't object to my being there at all. Apprently the Security Service suspected Eugene was not the simple Naval Attaché he made himself out to be.

'Well,' said Stephen, 'We play a lot of bridge at my club, the Connaught. Occasionally we have a meal together, and we meet for coffee up the road.'

'He's never asked you to put him in touch with anyone you know? Or for information of any kind?'

'No, he hasn't. But if he did, naturally I would get in touch with you straight away.'

The little man eyed Stephen dispassionately.

'If there's anything I can do,' Stephen continued, 'I'd be only too pleased to.'

'Carry on the relationship as you have been, as though nothing has happened.'

'Well, I'll let you know as soon as Eugene gets suspicious,' Stephen promised, as the man left.

'You wouldn't believe, little baby, that he was a cloak and dagger man, would you?' Stephen laughed.

'How about the bowler?' I giggled.

'And the little brief-case, and rolled umbrella?'

'Not to mention the glasses, National Health, I bet. And he couldn't have been more than four foot eleven!'

'But isn't it exciting, little baby? You know he really had a dagger under his mackintosh?'

We carried on sending him up, it was a good laugh. But neither of us was really impressed. The whole thing seemed a huge joke.

Stephen and Eugene used to discuss East/West relations. Russia had become very powerful, building up control over more and more of Eastern Europe. America, Britain

73

and France were planning within NATO to supply West Germany with nuclear war-heads which were going to be taken in by NATO troops. For months Berlin had been the focus of attention. Khruschev wanted to force the Allies to leave West Berlin and bring in Soviet troops. Russia desperately needed to know when the war-heads would arrive.

Russia tried to woo Britain and France away from America. The French government was riddled with Communist sympathisers. Over here, Henry Houghton, Winifred Gee and the Krogers were busy selling nuclear secrets to Russia, whilst William Vassall, a clerk at the Admiralty, had been discovered spying for the Russians. America was wondering whether Europe could be trusted. And yet, in that fraught atmosphere, it never occured to Stephen or me that our own tragedy was brewing.

* * * * *

People have said that Stephen led a depraved and dissolute existence, but during the time I knew and lived with him, though he could hardly be described as a paragon of virtue, he was always a kind, sympathetic father-figure, and he said that he deplored prostitution.

Stephen's girlfriends – and he had many – came to him for help and advice. Whatever the individual circumstances, the essence of Stephen's advice was always:

'Follow your instincts and desires.'

His closest friends were usually young girls who had been badly treated by men.

'You've got to stand up for yourself in this world,' he told them. 'Don't take any notice of him, just because he's a man.'

Stephen would have been a good suffragette. He firmly believed in equal rights for women. If anything, he believed that women were more intelligent, certainly more in control of their mental faculties than men, who he generally described as; 'Dirty little bastards, following their pricks.'

Stephen helped me, as he had done other girls, to make my way in life. There had been Maureen Swanson, who had married the Earl of Dudley; Margaret Brown, a top international model who later married the composer Jule Styne; Eunice Bailey, who married the son of the millionaire Sir Harry Oakes; not to mention Vickie Barrett, whose lies at Stephen's trial were more than he could bear.

I knew very little about the other girls, and naturally I didn't see myself in the same class as them. Stephen constantly referred to Maureen in public, telling stories about her sadistic antics. He certainly thought they owed their success to him, and to a large extent they did.

Stephen didn't believe that class distinction should prevent attractive and intelligent girls from humble backgrounds appearing in society. The rosebuds of the English aristocracy were so often highly-bred neurotics incapable of little more than becoming bitchy old women who wiled away life arranging flowers and ordering the servants about.

England at the beginning of the 'Sixties was still terribly prudish and riddled with class consciousness. Stephen was used to freer ways. He had taken his osteopathy degree in the United States, which was pretty classless, and had then worked as a tourist guide in Paris where it was accepted that men had mistresses. The hypocricy of the middle-class British was to drive the prostitutes off the streets in a feeble attempt to pretend they didn't exist. Meanwhile, sex orgies flourished behind the doors of the grandest homes.

Dukes and Ministers fought side by side with sadists, masochists, homosexuals and lesbians against the barriers of a frustrated society.

Stephen was bored. He began taking me for late-night drives round Paddington, searching the streets for prostitutes. We used to watch the girls round the all-night launderettes in Westbourne Park Road.

A black girl came out of her front door and walked towards the launderette. She went up to a big black guy, pulled out a wad of notes from her purse and handed them to him. He grinned and shrugged. Looking round the launderette, he muttered something before nodding at her to leave.

We watched her walking along the pavement of Westbourne Park Road, then Stephen started the engine and followed her in the car.

'She's sure to notice.' I worried.

Another prostitute peered through some broken basement railings.

'Fuck off, you black bastard, unless you want trouble,' she shouted. Our girl sneered, only holding her head higher, and walked on. Anyone looking for fun that nigh would obviously have chosen her. The basement prostitute was way past being able to entice anyone, unless he was so dead drunk he wouldn't have noticed the chalky make-up, the dried and withered skin, let along the bugs and diseases she must have carried.

'D'you think she's like that all over?' Stephen laughed. 'Why don't you go and ask her whether she's creased all over?'

I would do most things for Stephen to give him a kick, but that was one thing I couldn't do. The girl we were following found a pick-up, but didn't seem to like the look of him much, though he thrust a couple of quid in front of her nose. He looked like a rat in his shabby raincoat and round, thick-lensed specs. He was the type with a drip on the end of his nose. Then she spotted a large, probably Irish, man walking along the other side of the road. You could tell she was after him, although he didn't seem to take any notice of her.

'I'll bet you ten bob she doesn't make him,' said Stephen.

The fellow halted as they passed on opposite sides of the street. It was just beginning to rain. He crossed, and they went off together.

'Why don't you have a go?' Stephen laughed.

'You're crazy!'

'I don't mean seriously, silly. Why don't you just walk up the road and see how many men try to pick you up?'

'What for?'

'It'll be a kick. We'll take bets on it.'

'I'm not walking along this road alone.'

'No, not this one. I know, we'll do it on Notting Hill Gate. You can walk to the milk machine. I'll give you sixpence. I'll park the car a little way off and you can waggle your bottom and trip along to get some milk.'

'What if I'm stopped by the police?'

'Oh, just say you're going to get some milk and meeting me here.'

'OK.' I agreed. So we drove to within about a hundred yards of the machine and parked. I got out and walked off, a bit frightened. Two or three cars stopped, but I just kept my head high, and walked on. A little half-caste tried to pick me up on the way back, but I ignored him.

As I got near the car, I could see Stephen was laughing. Suddenly a voice close behind said:

'Darling.'

I quickened my pace to get to the safety of the car when

77

a hand touched my shoulder. Luckily, I reached Stephen and as I turned to get into the car, the man backed off angrily as we sped off, Stephen delighted with the whole game.

Notting Hill Gate was pretty rough then. You never knew when a fight might break out or a full-blown riot would erupt on the streets. A lot of the whites living there were convicts, pimps and prostitutes. Throw in a lot of generally misplaced people of assorted age, colour and nationality and you got trouble. It was Rachman land, and Stephen loved it.

He used to hang out with the black lawyers and writers at a little restaurant off Harrow Road, near where the Grand Union canal heads west from Little Venice past All Soul's Cemetery and the gasometers. The restaurant was in one of those streets where the rubbish was cleared only once a week and children ran barefoot searching the local pubs for their mothers.

From the window we watched the tramps from the canal looking for fag ends amongst piles of old car tyres. Sometimes a fight broke out in the street. Somebody would eventually pick up a bottle and smash it over another guy's head. Then the ambulance would come. Whatever time of day or night you were there, the police sirens wailed, never very far away.

Stephen always took his sketchbook to draw the West Indians. Sitting amongst all those black faces was quite a new and exciting thing to do then. It made a great impression on me, and Stephen seemed as happy there as anywhere. He was so adaptable. It didn't seem to matter where he was or what was going on. He always fitted in, he knew just what to do. Having always thought that all black men were bus conductors or road sweepers, it was a nice surprise to find out how wrong I and all those entrenched middle-class opinions were. These guys were getting on in the world. They had ideas, and they weren't going to let anything get in their way.

Stephen got a hang-up about the coloured girls he was drawing and joked how it would be fun to take one to bed. As usual, I was the one who was supposed to find her. I pointed out a vast black woman waddling along the pavement with a bundle of washing.

'What about her? Shall I run out and invite her in?'

'No!' said Stephen, leaping up to stop me rushing out of the door after her. 'I'd never be able to find it to put it in!'

The West Indian scene was something new for Stephen to tell everyone about. Stephen spent half his life meeting and being with people, and the other half he spent telling people about the other people he knew. He promised his friend Vasco Lazzolo, the society portrait artist, that it would be worth the trip.

'You've no idea what it's like there! There's always something going on. Come and see life in Paddington, Vasco. You're always reading about the race riots, come and see it for yourself.'

We were hoping for a good brawl that night, something worth talking about. Unfortunately, when we got to our restaurant, it was practically empty, which was a big let-down. But we'd noticed another, even seedier place, the El Rio Café, just up the road, and moved on there. We couldn't disappoint Vasco – Stephen's reputation would have been ruined.

The new restaurant didn't know us, and literally every-one in it was black. They stared at us as if we were from outer space, but left us in peace. We ordered some coffee and sat down, to look round. It seemed pretty uninterest-ing. There was nothing going on at all. We finished our coffee.

'I think they're smoking pot somewhere,' said Stephen, 'There's a musty smell wafting around.'

'What's it like?' we asked Stephen.

'I shouldn't think it has much effect,' Stephen answered. 'It probably depends on your attitude.'

We looked at some of the glazed expressions on people's faces.

'I wonder if they sell it here.'

'Well they certainly wouldn't sell it to us,' said Vasco. 'They'd think we were the law.'

I thought it might improve the evening if we got some. I would have done anything to put things right for Stephen, who was obviously disappointed that he hadn't been able to impress Vasco.

'I'll see if I can get some,' I said, wanting to show I wasn't scared of anything.

'OK, little baby, we'll wait outside for you in the car.'

'What do I ask for?'

'Grass or weed.'

I headed towards the toilets, and spotted a likely looking West Indian guy leaning against the wall in the passage.

'Hi there, baby,' he drawled. 'Going some place??'

He was wearing an open neck shirt, had little hair on his head but a neat beard and moustache. I hesitated.

'I'm looking for someone.'

'How 'bout you an' me tonight?' He opened his mouth a little and ran his tongue over his teeth.

'My friends are upstairs, waiting. I'm trying to find someone who will sell me some weed.'

He looked a bit surprised.

'How much?'

'How does it come?'

'Poun', ten shillin',' he raised a bored eyebrow.

'I'll take ten shillings worth,' offering him the note.

He disappeared down the stairs and returned a few minutes later with a scruffy piece of paper. Inside was a tiny amount of grassy looking things. I made a face, wondering if I'd been had.

'Going now, baby?' He stepped back into his position against the wall, but his hand blocked my exit.

'I've got to go, my brother's waiting.'

He touched my arm. 'Tomorrow, then?'

It occurred to me that Stephen would be delighted if I succeeded in fixing him up with a black girl.

'Well,' I said casually, 'we might be able to meet. But have you got a sister for my brother?'

'Sure thing, baby.' He smiled. 'Plenty of them. Tomorrow, then?'

'Well, I don't know. Look, I'll give you my telephone number. You can ring me when you've found a girl.'

He moved his arm and let me pass after I'd given him the number.

'See you, then.'

I smiled back at him and rushed upstairs to the car.

'I've got some.' I giggled and handed over the paper. 'And, guess what, Stephen? The man that sold it to me – you don't get much for ten shillings do you? – he's going to telephone us tomorrow. He said he'd find you one of his sisters! What do you think of that, Stephen? You've always said you wondered whether it was any different!'

'Great, little baby. How did you manage that?' Stephen was laughing again.

'You see what a great little girl I've got here? She finds girls for me, don't you, little baby? Shall I rent her to you for a week, Lazzolo? When do I meet my new friend, then?' He said, turning back to me.

'He's ringing tomorrow, we could all go out together, couldn't we?'

'Great idea. Then we'll learn what it's all about. And this was the same man who got the grass for you?'

'Yes.'

'Well, let's go home now and smoke it. How about that? What an exciting evening it's turned out to be.' Stephen and Lazzolo laughed pompously at me.

Back at the flat, we tried the grass.

'No effect whatsoever.' Stephen declared. 'Absolutely no effect.' I, meanwhile, had relaxed totally and couldn't stop laughing. It had really gone to my head.

8

LUCKY

TWO DAYS later I answered the 'phone to Lucky Gordon, the West Indian from the El Rio. His real name was Aloysius and he was thirty-one when I met him. He had left Jamaica thirteen years earlier, and apparently he was called 'Lucky' because his parents had won some money in a sweepstake on the day he was born. I found out later that he had been convicted for larceny, rape, grievous bodily harm and that he had been deported from Denmark. He certainly wasn't very lucky for me.

'I found my sister for your friend,' he said. 'And you come to a party tonight. I'll meet you at the café, all right?'

'Shove your money down the front of your dress,' Lucky told me, as he led Stephen and I down the ill-lit staircase into the damp, musty basement. What a weird place! All kinds of crazy things were going on in the dark. Dim brown bodies were writhing to the incessant throb of the jazz drum.

Lucky introduced Stephen to a coloured girl, but he didn't seem particularly interested in her. A kitchen led off from the main living-room where beer flowed from a barrel. Coloured boys, stripped from the waist up, urinated in the sink. No one talked much. They danced and clapped and jumped about, like animals, There were a few whites. Anaemic little men, washed-out civil servants or ponces, tried making up to the better-looking white chicks. Two white broads with pasty faces and peroxide hair perched dryly on their shoulders, stood around waiting for a pick-up.

Lucky had taken charge of me. He was terribly proud.

'This is my girl,' he would say. But before I had a chance to say anything, he'd drag me away to show me off to someone else.

As the music grew softer, the swaying bodies flopped to the floor and the joints were passed around. People smoked and joked with one another in one corner. In another they drank and sang and danced to the rhythm. I soon felt my head spinning from the mixture of cannabis and alcohol. My legs felt wobbly and I had to lean against a wall to steady myself. I tried to catch what Stephen was saying to me. But there didn't seem to be enough air to breathe. I felt as though I was floating into nothingness. It was totally different to when Stephen, Vasco and I had smoked our bit of grass and everything had been easy going for me.

Now I felt myself sinking to the ground. Stephen was beside me in a moment.

'Get her upstairs, Lucky. 'I'll bring the car round to the door.'

Lucky carried me over his shoulders. I recovered sufficiently in the fresh air to feel his hand slipping down my bra, searching for my money. I kicked at him to put me down, just as Stephen brought the car round.

'She's not well, Lucky. Come on, Christine. I've got the car here.' Stephen tried to lead me away, but Lucky was still holding on to me.

'I'll come with you then.'

'There's not enough room,' said Stephen. It was true, he was driving a two-seater.

84

'She's coming with me then, in a taxi,' Lucky insisted, jumping in front of me, so that I couldn't get into the car. Stephen was losing his cool.

'Can't you see she's not well?' he snapped, trying to move Lucky away.

The rush of adrenalin and cool air had almost restored me and, realising what was going on, I rushed round and jumped in on the driver's side.

'Look. I'm taking her,' Lucky persisted.

'Thank you Lucky. But I'm sure I'll be perfectly all right with Stephen.'

'I'll see you around,' Stephen added, having arranged with Lucky to get together with a dope peddlar in case any of his friends wanted any. It was just becoming fashionable to smoke, but still quite daring.

Every time the telephone rang after that we knew it would be Lucky. He kept asking me out and Stephen and I took it in turns to think up excuses for me. One day, when I had taken the call, Lucky wasn't that easily dissuaded.

'Look, I've got to see you.'

'I can't. I'm busy,' I said as usual.

'Listen, this is important. I've just got to see you.'

'I can't. I'm engaged, my boyfriend wouldn't like it.'

'You don't want to see me because I'm black, that's it isn't it?'

'No.'

'It's always the same with you lot. Too proud to be seen with a black guy.'

'No. That's not true. I've got a boyfriend already, and I can't see you as well.'

'I know it's because I'm black,' he shouted.

'No, no. I promise it's not.'

I didn't know what to say. I knew it was all wrong that people shouldn't mix because of their colour. But when it

85

came down to it, that was why I didn't want to see him. And I couldn't tell him. I was so confused and upset, I started crying.

'Hey, baby. Take it easy. I just want to see you for a minute. I got something I got to tell you.'

His voice had changed. It was soft and silky. He didn't want to upset me.

'What is it? Please Lucky. I'm tired, just leave me alone.'

'Just see me for coffee. Just one coffee, OK?'

'Oh, all right. Just for coffee.' I thought: that way he won't think I don't want to see him because he's black.

'I'll meet you in the café in Westbourne Park Road,' I suggested, not wanting to bump into anyone I knew. My mother would have died if she discovered I'd been talking to a black man.

I arrived at six o'clock, but Lucky wanted to take me off somewhere else.

'I want to show you something, at my place.'

'What is it?'

'Some jewellery.'

'What jewellery?'

'Some I stole. I want to get rid of it, see?'

Stephen and I knew a few crooks. Maybe they would be interested. There seemed no harm in it, so I agreed to have a look.

* * * * *

We walked up hundreds of stairs, him following me.

'Keep going, baby.'

At last he opened the door to his flat and closed it behind us.

'Keep on going, through there.'

86

I did as he said and found myself in his bedroom. I was just about to ask where the jewellery was when I realised he had closed the door and was standing back against it, a small knife in his hand.

My mind went blank.

'What do you mean, Lucky?' I was quite numb. I wasn't even able to think of all the rape and murder stories one hears about. That came later. Now I just stared at him. He was peering at me, his eyes hard and cold, the look of a madman.

He came towards me, slowly.

'Don't be silly, Lucky. Where are the jewels you were talking about?'

'Look, Lucky. I think I had better go home.'

He flicked open the knife as I moved towards the door.

'Now, look here, Lucky. You can't do . . .'

'Take off your dress,' he ordered, holding the opened knife forward and undoing the buttons on his shirt with his free hand.

The first thing I thought was that he'd rip my dress if I didn't take it off. There was obviously no way I could make a run for it. I took the dress off.

He held the knife to my throat. He forced me back on to the bed and pulled off my knickers. He was naked too, and when I tried to argue he got more excited, as was plain to see. With the knife in one hand, he had me.

Afterwards, I jumped up and grabbed my dress, thinking that was that.

'Stay there!' he shouted.

'What for?'

'You're staying where you are!'

'What d'you mean? You've had what you wanted. You lied about the jewellery. What more d'you want? Are you going to kill me with that silly little knife?' The knife I knew was sharp enough to slit my throat, no trouble at all.

'You're staying here.'

'Not if you don't get rid of that knife.'

I couldn't believe the situation. There was something quite pathetic seeing him standing there naked with the knife in his hand. He went out of the room and locked the door.

I'd no idea how long he'd be gone or what was going to happen. I looked round the room, but there was no way out, and if he had a telephone it was in another room. Before I had time to do anything else, Lucky came back. He threw the knife on the floor as I pulled a dirty grey blanket over me. There weren't even any sheets on the bed and the whole place smelt stale.

'Uncover yourself!'

I just pulled the blankets closer.

'Stephen will be going mad, he'll be expecting me at home.'

Lucky picked up the knife and toyed with it in his lean, brown hands.

'You uncover yourself. Look, do what I say and you won't get hurt.'

He threw the knife gently from hand to hand. He was getting excited again. Surely, he wasn't going to do it again. He'd only just done it.

'Why are you keeping me here? What are you going to do with me?' I panicked. The full horror of the situation was beginning to filter through. He had been waiting for this and, seizing his chance, he moved deliberately towards me and then with a quick flick of the blade, tumbled the blanket onto the floor.

His eyes and the knife hypnotised me. I preferred to watch the knife rather than his piercing eyes. He ran the blade lightly across my calf. I still couldn't look at him. I felt that the hatred would have shown. If I tried to defy him, maybe even fight him, I knew instinctively that he would have killed me. The passionate loathing he had was so strong. He wanted power over me, to see me in his control and I had to go along with that, in order to save myself.

Again he tossed the knife aside, and like a maniac threw himself onto me, pumping himself into me. I knew resistance would only anger and excite him, so I lay there passively, waiting for his monstrous energy to subside.

He rolled beside me and lay there, panting.

'Are you going to let me go, now?'

'There's no need to talk that way. Didn't you enjoy it?'

'No.'

'But, look,' he pleaded softly. 'We could be happy together.'

'Yes, maybe,' I said, thinking this might be the only way to get round him. If I told him the truth – 'No. Never, I hate you. Let me go!' – He would have slashed me, cut my stomach, my throat, till the blood surged and there would be this animal having sex with a corpse.

'I've got to telephone Stephen. He'll be worried.'

Lucky still ignored me, turning away and pretending to sleep, but still keeping a firm grip on my arm. It was pitch black outside. It could have been midnight or three in the morning. I'd lost all track of time.

After a while I heard him breathing steadily. Despite his bald head and narrow eyes he didn't look frightening anymore, and I was even moved to feel pity for him. But I was mainly trying to think of a way of getting out. I stirred, and instantly his muscles tensed, though he said nothing.

I looked towards the tiny window. Maybe I could squeeze through. There might be a balcony, or a ladder below. I could try that. Perhaps the door wasn't locked and I'd be able to get out that way. I would creep down all those stairs very, very quietly, because Lucky had told me that all the people in the house were cousins or close friends of his.

I lay there and planned my escape. After I reckoned enough time had gone by, I edged my left leg gently towards the side of the bed and felt the cold air on my toes. Still his breathing continued. I waited again in that position, staring at my dress on the floor, wondering whether I would have time to put it on. Slowly I moved my toes to the floor, but as they touched the cold, dirty linoleum, Lucky sat bolt upright and with one swift movement, clamped me down. I was too upset to cry. I wanted to cry, but I couldn't. Eventually, I must have slept from nervous exhaustion.

*   *   *   *   *

The next day there was no respite. As soon as he woke he had me again. I started to cry, but he liked that.

'I want to go to the toilet.' I did, but I also thought I might have a chance to look around, see where I was. He could hardly refuse my request, so he got out of bed. He wouldn't let me get dressed, but dragged me with him to the lavatory and stood outside the door, which made it jolly difficult to go. I pulled the chain and came out, only to be taken straight back to the bedroom. It was like being a dog.

'I've never been away from Stephen for such a long time,' I said, not looking at him, in case he saw how frightened I was.

'Please, let me at least telephone him to tell him I'm all right. Please, please?'

I smiled at him and put my arms out towards him, trying to look as pathetic as I felt. I tried humbleness, so that he'd think he'd won, that I was his. But he decided not to give in straight away, and continued his bizarre love-making for a few more hours. I pretended I was enjoying myself, in order to get him on my side. Finally he went next-door into his friend's room, and brought the telephone back with him on a long extension.

I dialled Stephen's number. Luckily he was in the office.

'Where have you been, naughty baby? I've been worried about you.'

'Oh, I'm all right. I'm at Lucky's.' I hoped by the tone of my voice he'd realise I was in trouble. He did and said very loudly,

'Well, you'd better get home in half an hour.'

'All right, Stephen. I'll be right back.' I replaced the receiver and told Lucky Stephen had ordered me home.

'If I don't go, he'll be over here to get me.'

'He doesn't know where I live.'

'He could find out from the café. I know how possessive he is. He'll send the police round,' I said, not realising how much that was going to frighten Lucky. It was the only thing that he was scared of, *really* scared.

But still he wouldn't let me go.

'I'll come back,' I lied in my jolliest voice. He just shrugged.

'I promise. I must go now. Don't you see? Stephen will hit the roof. He might do anything, and we don't want any trouble. You must understand. Stephen wouldn't like it. He's very snobbish and doesn't understand that coloured people are the same as everyone else.'

Lucky looked at me with loathing.

'And nor did I, until I got to know you,' I hastily added. 'Naturally, I was frightened of you. Don't you understand?

English girls are brought up to think of coloured people as bogey men, something evil. It's not my fault that I was frightened of you at first.'

'But you're not frightened of me now, are you?'

'No, no of course not and I'd very much like to see you again.'

'You promise you'll come back?'

'Yes, of course I promise.'

Now that Stephen knew where I was, I was no longer frightened. I felt so completely exhausted, it was difficult to say anything at all. I could see he was beginning to believe that I cared about him, and while I carried on convincing him, I was slowly getting dressed. At last he said he'd let me go.

'I'll telephone you in an hour,' he said.

'Well, I think I'll go to sleep straight away, I hardly slept at all last night.'

'I'll telephone you in an hour,' he repeated.

I lingered on, even after he said he'd let me go, investing a few minutes of my life, just to make sure I got down those stairs and out of the front door without any hitches.

'Well, I'd better go now. Stephen'll be frantic,' I said finally, trying to sound sad that I had to leave. And just to show that I wasn't mad with him I gave him a warm kiss. He responded like a baby and cheered up a bit.

Before he knew it, I was saying, 'Goodbye. See you soon,' and walking slowly down the stairs, out of the front door and onto the dirty street. Hundreds of ordinary people were wandering around as they do every day of the week. I walked casually, as though nothing unusual had happened. But when I got round the corner I started running. I grabbed the first taxi I saw and went straight to Stephen and told him all about it.

'Oh, Stephen. I was terrified. I'm lucky to be alive. You

just don't know what he did. I've been there for eighteen hours. Do you realise I thought I would never get out? It was awful.'

Stephen put his arm round me to comfort me.

'Oh dear, well at least you're home and safe now. The trouble is I don't think there's going to be much we can do about it. We'll have to forget this one. There's no point in taking up proceedings, we'd have the entire population of Paddington against us. Besides, little baby, you were lucky there weren't six of them. I've heard they go for gang bangs quite a bit. There was a case in the papers not long ago.'

He was right, of course. There was nothing else to do but be thankful it hadn't been worse. Unfortunately, neither Stephen nor I realised that this was just the beginning. By making Lucky think that I really did like him, I had got myself into even more trouble. It couldn't have been more than half an hour before the 'phone rang. Stephen answered and I heard him telling Lucky I was busy. I think that although Stephen still treated the whole thing as a bit of a joke, he was beginning to think Lucky was pretty crazy.

That afternoon Sir Oswald Mosely had an appointment to see Stephen. Throughout their conversation Stephen would answer the telephone.

'She doesn't want to speak to you, Lucky,' he repeated and slammed down the receiver.

'What's going on?' enquired Mosely.

'Someone worrying Christine.'

It couldn't have been more than five minutes after Mosely had left that the doorbell rang. I looked out of the window to see who it was.

'It's Lucky!'

'Well, thank the Lord, Oswald Mosely's left!'

'Why?'

'Lucky probably would have shot him. The blacks can't stand what he's up to. They've been out for his blood for some time.'

'What shall I do, Stephen? I can't let him in.'

Stephen got up and said rather pompously:

'I've had enough of this pestering. Let him in, Christine. We'll soon see what's what. Much better have it out with him face to face. Tell him, in front of me, that you don't want to have anything further to do with him.'

Stephen really wasn't much good at playing the stern father unless he was really angry, and he laughed and added in a calmer tone:

'Any reasonable person will see that he can't go on like this.'

Reasonable person?

I went downstairs and let him in. With Lucky was the coloured dope-dealer Stephen had met at the blues party.

'Look,' said Lucky walking towards Stephen, talking man to man. 'I want a word with her privately.'

'All right, but make it quick.'

Lucky followed me into the bedroom, but then he locked the door and dragged me on to the bed.

'Stephen!' I managed to scream before Lucky put his hand over my mouth. Stephen and the other man rushed to the door and starting banging on it. But Lucky, wild-eyed, took no notice.

I took my chance and just prayed it would work.

'For Christ's sake! Let me go, Lucky!' I yelled. 'You're just being stupid. Don't you realise that Stephen will call the police?'

Very slowly and deliberately he released my arm and sat cowering like a cornered animal. I leapt to the lock and turned the key and Stephen fell into the room.

'How dare you behave like this in my house!' he raged. 'We are all going to talk this out properly. Make us some coffee, Christine.'

I did, as usual, as I was told. On my return, Stephen said,

'Now tell him in front of me.'

I knew what he meant.

'I don't want to see you again, Lucky.' I said calmly, standing beside Stephen. 'I've got another boyfriend.'

But Lucky didn't hear me. He didn't want to. He jumped up – it was amazing how the pace of his actions changed in a flash – and was suddenly grabbing me by the throat and shaking me.

Stephen and the other guy pulled him off and dragged him down the stairs as Lucky struggled and screamed;

'I got to talk to her! I got to talk to her!'

I followed them.

'Just let me whisper to her,' he said between wild kicks.

'Look I won't touch her. I just wanna whisper something.'

I went alongside them and whilst they held him off, he whispered;

'You must see me again.'

'Yes, yes.' I said. *Anything* to pacify him and get him out. His eyes were still wild.

When they had left, Stephen immediately telephoned the police and told them that a seemingly crazed drug-addict had locked me up for eighteen hours in his house and then come round to Stephen's place and tried to carry right on there. The police came round and took our statements, but as there were no marks on me, they couldn't prosecute. They told me to go to the doctor's to make sure I hadn't caught anything.

The next day Stephen 'phoned Scotland Yard, as

agreed, to let them know whether Lucky was still pestering me.

'Hey, little baby, if we were to go round to Scotland Yard, they might just show us the Black Museum. I'd love to see that. All sorts of weapons, whips and things. The actual things that people used against each other!'

We never went, though. It was just another of Stephen's fleeting ideas.

Lucky continued ringing, and we considered changing the number. Although we seldom saw him, if we were coming home late we drove into the garage with the headlights on and ran upstairs as quickly as possible.

Me by the pool at Cliveden, where it all began.

Stephen Ward in a relaxed moment.

Mandy Rice-Davies leaving the Old Bailey.

John Profumo and his wife Valerie Hobson.

Eugene Ivanov in his Russian naval uniform.

Lucky Gordon trying to get at me outside the Old Bailey.

Joanne Whalley as me in the film *Scandal*.

Me reading the Government version. Justice?!?

9

JACK

THAT SUMMER we sweltered in a heatwave, and Stephen and I spent as much time as possible at the cottage. I sunbathed while Stephen did the gardening, which he loved. Nearly every weekend some of Stephen's friends came to stay. When he wasn't using it himself, Bill Astor allowed Stephen full use of the walled swimming-pool not far from the main house. I'd loved playing in the water ever since the days when I swam with the boys from home in the Wraysbury quarry pits, and diving into the pool at Cliveden was one of my greatest pleasures that summer.

One hot Friday evening, after a sticky week in London, I arranged to meet a Persian friend called Leon Norell in a club for a few drinks. Stephen had suggested that I pick up a girl for him and drive down to Cliveden with the two of them for a swim and a bit of a party later on. Stephen was not averse to asking me this kind of favour. I was his little tool for getting girls. Not only that, but he wanted me in the room when he was making love to them and, if they stayed the night, he would ask me to sleep between them afterwards.

It was hot and sticky in London that night. Wherever we went the clubs smelt of stale alcohol and sweat. Although I hadn't found a girl for Stephen, we decided we had to leave the city. What a relief it was to feel the cool wind blowing on our faces. Driving past London Airport, we offered a lift to a girl waiting at the bus stop. She seemed nice, so we invited her to the party at Stephen's cottage.

The three of us pulled up outside the cottage. After a few drinks we rushed up to the swimming-pool. I had left my bathing costume behind, so I borrowed one of the many lying around. It didn't fit very well and Stephen dared me to take it off, which of course I did. Stephen was the first to notice Bill Astor coming through the gate with a guest, John Profumo. Although I didn't know it, he was the Secretary of State for War. As usual, Stephen quickly thought up a brilliant idea to liven up the party: he whipped my bathing costume from the side of the pool and flung it out of reach into the hedge.

'Now you're in for it, little baby!'

'You devil! Give it back!'

'What are you going to do now?' Stephen was delighted.

By now, everyone was standing around the pool laughing. I spotted a damp bit of towelling lying beside the pool, and swam quickly across to it before the others could get there and snatch away my only hope of escape. It was impossible to get out at the deep end decently, so I dragged the pitiful piece of towel with me to the shallow end. I only just managed to wrap it round me and get out, and I was barely decent.

But the fun had only just begun. No sooner was I out of the water than Bill and John Profumo started chasing me. I ran nimbly round the pool with the pair of them in tow, both trying to grab at my towel. It was very funny, until I stubbed my toe. Bill had the bright idea of turning on the floodlights for a better view, and in the light I could see Stephen, shaking with laughter.

We all sobered up a bit when we heard the voices of Bill's other guests approaching. It was embarrassing to be formally introduced to ladies in tiaras and long evening dresses and gentlemen in tails whilst I, with my hair soaking wet, looked more like a water sprite with just a square of towelling across my front. Somehow I succeeded in shaking hands with a couple of them before excusing myself to change.

After we had dressed, we went up to join the other guests in the big house. There was quite a crowd, about thirty people, including Ayub Khan, the President of Pakistan, Lord and Lady Dalkeith, a scattering of Conservative MPs and, of course, John Profumo and his wife, the actress Valerie Hobson.

Cliveden was used to providing entertaining diversions from the heavy affairs of state, and that weekend was no exception. Russia was threatening to march her troops into West Berlin and Ayub Khan was on his way to Washington to discuss the crisis. Profumo had had a heavy week being hounded by the British press and George Wigg, the Labour MP with a keen interest in the Army, after it's embarrassing defeat in Kuwait. Even Macmillan and the Government were coming under a certain amount of flack from the public for not delivering the good times they had promised.

I wasn't very interested in any of the guests except for the man I had met by the pool. He looked determined, someone who knew his own mind, and he was quite obviously bright. I was pleased when 'Jack' Profumo noticed me and asked if I would like to see round the house.

Passage after passage, room after room – it was even more enormous inside than I imagined Buckingham Palace to be. It wasn't somewhere I should like to live – it was so distant and must have been freezing in winter, the rooms were so large. Jack started getting excited about ever reaching the end. As room led onto room, I rushed on to the next door.

'This has just got to be the last!'

It quickly turned into a game. He started chasing me round the desks and tables. Every time he caught me, he tried to kiss me. We found some suits of armour standing in the hall and, just for a joke, I put one on. It was far too big and clanked whenever I tried to move. I caused an uproar when I paraded before the others – everyone fell about laughing. I'm quite certain that for a few hours that evening, those Members of Parliament and diplomats forgot their worldly problems.

After the party, my friend drove back to London and dropped off the girl we had picked up. I stayed the night at the cottage with Stephen and the next morning, on our way back to London, we dropped in at the main house to fix Bill's back. Whilst Stephen was doing that, I chattered to his wife Bronwen. Afterwards we set off for London to pick up two of Stephen's girlfriends. All that month he had managed to keep these two affairs apart, but now he was in a fix. He had invited both girls down to the cottage on the same day. He rang Eugene Ivanov and asked him to come along too, hoping that the Russian would take care of one of them. As it happened, things didn't turn out like that at all.

Bill Astor had invited us back again for a swim, and while we were getting ready to leave London, Stephen and I discussed how best to handle the two girls. How was he going to explain one to the other? The fact that I was going didn't really matter – I was always introduced and accepted by all Stephen's girlfriends as his 'little baby'. In the end we decided there was nothing to be done but to make the best of the situation. I would keep both girls happy by telling both of them, 'Well, I know he likes you best.' It worked a treat.

We all set off from London in two cars, Eugene following Stephen, as this was Eugene's first visit to Cliveden. When we arrived at the estate we went straight to the pool, where Lord Astor's friends were gathered. A few of Stephen's friends, who had just turned up on the spur of the moment, as they so often did, were also beside the pool. We all joined up to splash around in the pool. Jack, Eugene, Ayub Khan and Bill Astor got in the deep end and raced each other to the shallow end – without using their legs. I'll never forget how Stephen laughed and laughed at Jack, who was cheating by walking the last bit. Of course he won the race easily. Even Eugene laughed when Jack said,

'That'll teach you to trust the British!'

After the men's race it was mixed doubles. A girl climbed onto each man's shoulders – I was on Jack's – and the winner was the pair who managed to stay afloat the longest. I don't think anyone won as we were all flapping about, falling off and sinking at the same time. It was great fun, and the afternoon passed quickly.

Sometimes it was nice being in London while Stephen was away, so I decided to drive home that evening with Eugene, who had to return to the Russian Embassy. Before I left, Jack Profumo asked me for my telephone number.

'I live with Stephen. Ask him for the number,' I said, thinking that would be the end of that. I was reluctant to give it to him – he was a bit too pushy for my liking.

Eugene and I left early and headed off to London. He talked about Russia the whole way. At one point a car swerved dangerously in front of us. Eugene cursed the driver and got in a foul mood about it.

'We call them road hogs,' I said, trying to cheer him up. 'You know – a pig that pushes in front all the time. A pig – oink, oink.'

He didn't get the point. 'In Russia,' (Eugene began every statement 'In Russia . . .'), 'You are simply stopped there and then, and a mark is made in your driving book. Once you have three such marks you automatically cease to drive. Much better system, don't you think?'

'Yes, I suppose so,' I agreed. It would never have done to argue with Eugene.

'In Russia the system is better. No court cases – just three warnings.'

'Do you have houses like Cliveden, in Russia?'

'Naturally,' he replied sullenly. 'In Russia though, such places are for the use of all, but then in Russia we have adopted a different system of government. It is much better, you see. We don't have the most popular person in control of a department of the interior – we have the most suitable. Naturally, the results are far better. In the West you choose someone to manage the building industry who may know nothing about it.'

So he continued, praising all things Russian and denigrating our British system. Nevertheless he fascinated me. He always had. He was very quiet, the kind of person I liked to try and arouse. So when he dropped me off at the house, I invited him in for a cup of coffee, but he had a better idea. From the boot of his car he produced a bottle of vodka.

'In Russia, we drink vodka.'

We drank and talked more about his country. He told me how large it was, how much had been achieved by the Party, how loyal its people were to Progress.

'In Russia, we don't have bus conductors,' he said very seriously. 'The people are trusted to pay. We don't have homosexuals in Russia either – we do not have that kind of person.'

After we had drunk most of the vodka, he suddenly

leant forward and kissed me. Before I knew what was happening, I was in his arms. He was a wonderful lover, so masculine. He left not long after and I felt a tremendous warmth about him: he was not the sort of man to do that sort of thing, and I could see he was sad to have weakened. He didn't come round for a few weeks after that but met Stephen elsewhere, and when he finally did show up at the house, he acted as though nothing had happened. What a man.

* * * * *

Stephen was in a tizz when he got back home the following morning.

'Guess what? Jack Profumo wanted your telephone number, so I gave it to him.'

I wasn't exactly enthralled.

'Well you know he's the War Minister, don't you?'

'What!' I couldn't believe it. I immediately wondered whether I had been suitably respectful.

'And did you enjoy yourself last night, little baby? What did you do with Eugene?'

'We talked.'

'What else did you do?' Stephen teased.

'Well, you know . . . I think he's great.'

'I don't *know*!' Stephen laughed. 'What with Eugene on the one hand and Jack on the other – we could start a war. So you had Eugene – you naughty little baby!'

'I think he was a bit sad afterwards,' I said, remembering how he had crept out ashamed, unable to look me in the eye.

'Why?'

'Well . . . he said they don't do things like that in Russia.'

Stephen collapsed in giggles.

'They don't do things like that in Russia! Don't they, little baby, don't they?'

'Anyway, Stephen, I like Russians, even if they are all spies. It's up to them, isn't it? We're all as bad as each other. All the same, I like him, whatever he is.' I defended poor Eugene, because Stephen was making such a joke of him.

'I expect he *is* a spy,' Stephen said peering at me. 'How exciting that would be, wouldn't it, little baby?'

* * * * *

Jack Profumo telephoned me the following day to ask whether I'd like to go for a drive. I accepted immediately. Now that I knew who he was, I was intrigued. I wanted to know what he was really like. Besides, I had nothing better to do that sweltering afternoon.

When Jack arrived, Stephen was on his way out to meet Eugene. They waved to each other politely and I climbed into Jack's shiny black car. I had never been in such a colossal car. The padded leather seats were sheer luxury. He drove me around and gave me a guided tour of London. We drove past Number 10 Downing Street, which I had never seen before and he pointed out the barracks he was in charge of, and the building where he worked. I was certainly impressed by his relaxed and easy manner. His eyes twinkled and he had an easy smile.

This was the beginning of The Profumo Affair. An affair! What *was* this affair that became tainted by the filthy minds of the creeps in their two-up two-down semi-detached suburbia? What was this 'impropriety' which became the talking-point of the world? Does the proof of impropriety lie between striped sheets? This was a brief affair, with little real communication. It had no more real meaning than a hand-shake or a look across a crowded room. But in the tiny minds of the people who see the world of intrigue through the eyes of James Bond, who see only cheap thrills in dark alleys, for them the act of sleeping with someone is tantamount to treachery.

Jack dropped me home.

'See you again?' I nodded.

'I'll ring you tomorrow then – but . . . er, I'd rather not run into Stephen.'

'Oh, but he's all right. He doesn't mind in the least who I see. He's just a friend of mine. It's not what you think – we just don't.'

'Yes, I know. But all the same, perhaps I could meet you somewhere else if he's at home. It's not personal – it's just better that way.'

I was rather surprised by his attitude, but I agreed. 'OK. Ring me first and I'll tell you if he's going to be in or not.'

Jack's big black car purred away as I closed the front door. Inside I found Stephen, lolling on the sofa, waiting for me.

'Well?' He raised an eyebrow mockingly. 'Well, what have you been up to this time?'

Stephen was always longing to know what I had been up to. It was almost as though he lived life second-hand. The moment I got in he bombarded me with questions: where had I been, who with, what had we done? Whenever Stephen and I weren't doing anything, we always talked about the people we had been doing something with, or laughing and joking about a plan to do something in the future.

'We went for a drive and he showed me where he worked and everything,' I said.

'Everything? Naughty little baby!'

I giggled. 'Stephen. You've got a dirty little mind and you always twist things. I really don't think I can go on living with you – I'll be contaminated!'

'When is he seeing you again?'

'He said he'd call,' I said impatiently.

'I don't know what's to become of you, Christine. You really are a naughty little baby. At this rate, we'll be running the world between us.'

'But Stephen, we didn't get up to anything.' I didn't realise then what Stephen was so excited about. As far as I was concerned, Jack Profumo was just another man. I didn't know that Stephen had already contacted the security services again. Then he told me about the meeting – he was terribly excited about it. He had told 'Mr Woods' that Eugene Ivanov and Jack Profumo had met at Cliveden that weekend and that, during his stay, Ivanov had asked Stephen if he knew when the Americans were going to give West Germany the bomb. Whatever he thought the outcome might be, Stephen was thoroughly enjoying the drama of it all.

'Two bottles of vodka were drunk,' he told Woods, exaggerating of course. 'This girl is very much in demand. Believe it or not – Mr Profumo asked me for her telephone number. I didn't like to refuse – it would have been rude – but I thought you ought to know. It might develop into a most awkward and dangerous situation.'

Stephen told me that MI5 had instructed him to avoid talking to Eugene about anything that might relate to the questions he had asked. Stephen assured them that he knew nothing anyway. Both Stephen and I had apparently been thoroughly checked by MI5 and Special Branch after Mr Woods' first visit, and of course nothing had been found against us. MI5 had told Stephen that as he knew

106

Eugene Ivanov they would bear him in mind as a useful contact should Ivanov want to defect, or in case Mr Profumo wished to meet the Russian socially.

That afternoon, Sue, an old friend of Stephen's, came round. She was in a very bad state. She had left her husband and was threatening to kill herself.

'Look, Sue,' Stephen told her, 'Suicide is the easy way out. It takes far more guts to live than to die.'

I made some coffee for them and brought it in.

'Honestly Sue, no man is worth it. Nor is any woman.' Stephen knew what he was talking about. He had tried to kill himself, when his first fiancée had let him down.

'Life is what you make it,' he persuaded her. 'Come on, I'll draw you.' He sat there drawing and chatting to her for ages, so I decided to go to bed.

I was fast asleep when I was awakened by Stephen opening the door. He was naked. 'Come on and see this, little baby. We've really got a very sexy creature here.'

I got up unwillingly and followed him into his bedroom. I didn't like to refuse him. Lying on the bed, quite nude, was the girl who had been so miserable.

'What shall I do to her, Christine?'

'Oh, I don't know,' I laughed – there wasn't much else I could do. Sue was laughing too. I left them to it, only to be called back later to sleep next to Stephen.

* * * * *

Jack telephoned me later that week, suggesting another drive. This time he turned up in a mini, and we drove off to his house near Regent's Park. It was a beautiful house.

'It comes with my job,' he explained. I wished then that my parents had a nice house to live in, for the caravan was falling to pieces. I had sworn that one day I would give my Mum a proper little house.

'It's very lovely,' I sighed.

'Have you a large family, any brothers and sisters?'

'No, none.'

'You must have been very spoilt then?'

'Yes,' I said. What I was actually thinking was how the caravan had only been connected with electricity and running water a few years ago, although my stepfather had worked as hard as this man did.

'Yes, I was the only child.'

We finished our drinks while chatting about the weekend at Cliveden.

'Come along, I'll show you the house.'

He showed me the dining room. 'We often have the Queen for dinner here.' I stared at the table.

'Gosh! How fantastic!' I tried to imagine her sitting there, eating.

On either side of the main staircase were two huge, ornamental dogs.

'My wife bought those,' he explained, as we walked upstairs to his office. There were at least three telephones on his desk, one of which looked most unusual.

'Oh, that's a scrambler. I use that if I want to 'phone the Prime Minister. No one except us can understand what we're saying.' Then he took me into the next room.

'This is the bedroom,' he said, as if it needed explanation. It was wonderful, the most glorious, luxurious room. I was bowled over. Jack was not terribly handsome, but he did have a strong personality and that afternoon he knew what he wanted. He was completely at ease, sure of himself, and I found myself unable to say no.

After that, we used to meet at Stephen's house, when he was out. Jack would try and buy me presents or give me money, but I had always refused. I didn't want his money. I felt that what feeling there was between us would have been debased if I took his money. But Jack seemed to want to give me something:

'You must want to buy yourself something,' he would say, digging into his pockets.

'No, I don't.'

'But there must be something you want.'

'There isn't. Honestly Jack, I don't want anything.'

'What about your mother?' he asked once.

'What do you mean?'

'Well, you could get something for your parents,' he suggested. Jack knew how poor my Mum and Dad were. 'Here, take this and buy something your mother needs, even if you don't want anything yourself.' So I accepted his twenty pounds, and gave some money to my mother that weekend. Thankfully, he never suggested giving me money again, but once he bought me a little lighter as a gift, which was much nicer.

* * * * *

The night after I had been to Jack's house, Stephen and I were lying in bed when he asked me about the bomb.

'What bomb?' I asked. I was quite innocent of world affairs, as I never read the papers or watched the news.

'The one America is supposed to be giving to West Germany. What with you knowing Eugene and Jack Profumo.'

It didn't sound particularly exciting to me.

'You could easily find out,' he said, 'from Jack.'

'Don't be silly, I couldn't do anything like that, Stephen. Jack would never discuss anything like that with me, anyhow.'

'Ha! Ha! I was only joking, little baby!' he laughed and turned over to go to sleep, still giggling to himself. 'Good-night.'

I was suspicious of Stephen and the following weekend in the garden at the cottage I blurted out,

'Stephen, I'm *sure* Eugene's a spy!'

'I'm sure he is too, but there's a lot of money in it, baby.' He laughed and carried on weeding, but I knew he was still thinking about it.

After Stephen had told the security people about Eugene's question, my affair with Jack Profumo came to an abrupt end. First he wrote to me saying that he couldn't see me as arranged, as something had suddenly cropped up which meant he had to leave town that evening. When we next met he made it quite clear that he could no longer see me in the present circumstances.

We were sitting in the car outside Stephen's flat when he brought the subject up:

'Why don't you get a flat on your own somewhere, Christine? I could find one for you.'

'Why?'

'Because I can't go on seeing you if you continue living here with Stephen,' he said, with no explanation. I couldn't understand what he had got against Stephen.

'But look,' I said, 'I don't have anything to do with Stephen. And even if I did – well, you don't own me, you know. You don't even mean that much to me. Why do you want to break up my relationship with Stephen? What's wrong with him?'

Jack didn't answer. I thought he was sulking, but of course the truth was that the security people, briefed by Stephen, had warned Jack that he was treading on dangerous ground. I was very upset.

'I don't understand!' I cried. 'You're just being jealous

and possessive, and if that's the way its going to be, we'd better forget it!'

It wasn't as if I loved him, although I did enjoy being with him and I liked going to bed with him.

'Well, I can't see you again if you remain here,' Jack repeated, after a moment's consideration. I, of course, knew nothing about the fact that the security people had warned Jack that he might be behaving indiscreetly, what with Eugene and Stephen and all the rest of it.

'All right then!' I shouted. 'Don't see me again!' And that was that. I got out, slammed the car door and, without looking back, slammed the front door. I was terribly hurt to think that he wouldn't have anything to do with me, just because I lived with Stephen. Stephen was my greatest friend and I wasn't going to leave him for someone who thought so badly of him. I went upstairs and cried, but I never told Stephen what Jack had said. If I had, it would only have ended in an argument. Stephen would have told me to go: 'Don't let me stand in your way.' He would have been upset and I would have had to comfort and reassure him that he was the only man that mattered to me. No, it was better that he should never know.

Jack wrote to me once, after that. He said that if I would like to see him again, I could get in touch. I didn't bother reading the letter twice, and I never saw him again.

Eugene Ivanov also kept his distance. Russians weren't the most popular people around at the time. On August 13th, 1961 they drove a wall slap bang through the middle of Berlin. They separated mothers from their children, brothers from sisters, and they shot innocent people who tried to get past it.

10

AXE

MANDY WAS delighted with her life with Peter Rachman, and became an expert in extracting the very most she could from him. She did like him a lot. Perhaps because he was the only person who showed any real interest in her. Unlike me, she never disobeyed him. She did, however, need an excuse to get away from him from time to time, and I was a good one as Peter still avoided me.

Stephen was going to the occasional orgy, but he was now rather bored with them. He always asked if I wanted to go along, but I refused. They didn't turn me on. One night though, when Mandy was with me at the flat, we agreed to pick him up after the party as he didn't have his car.

We arrived while the night was still young. The guests were bankers, brokers and professionals from Harley Street, plus a smattering of artists, for luck. The girls were young and very sexy. There was only one rule: never, on any account, have anything to do with another person privately. If a couple disappeared into a corner, they were quickly flushed out and jeered at. It wasn't sporting.

Stephen never joined in. He preferred watching or holding court in a corner, talking with people who had just finished themselves off. He was talking with some members of the bar about the publication of obscene books, a favourite topic of conversation as *Lady Chatterley's Lover* had just been published. *Lady C.* made the porno magazines passed round by the eminent bankers look like stories for the under-sevens.

It had been at one of these parties that Stephen met a girl called Valerie. She enjoyed masochist sex and Stephen actually became quite fond of her, even feeling a little upset that she went and married a barrister with even stronger sadistic tendencies!

* * * * *

Winter passed and Stephen started pottering about in his garden again. He talked a lot about the Russian way of life. I was doing very little modelling. My time disappeared in a whirl of shopping, cooking and looking after Stephen and his friends. I felt like an au-pair. Mandy was having problems with Peter. And the only real trouble in my life was Lucky Gordon.

I never knew when he would ring. Often he'd call in the middle of the night, demanding to see me. I never felt safe. I watched for him on the streets and kept glancing behind me when I went out. Stephen would try and get me to shake off my fear:

'Come on, baby. Let's go down to the jungle and hear the drums beat. You've got to live dangerously.'

I'd go with him, but we never stopped the car, just in case Lucky was around.

Stephen got the most out of the intrigue. In time everyone had heard about the 'dreadful maniac who forced his way in and attacked both of us'. One evening Alfred Marks and his wife arrived for a drink. As usual Stephen didn't have any, so he suggested that we went off to the El Rio:

113

'It'll be a real laugh. We'll see if Lucky Gordon's there – that's the wild man who attacked us. Honestly, you must see him for yourself.'

Stephen's plans always sounded so exciting that everyone would rush to take part. Alfred was soon jumping up, ready to go. When we arrived at the El Rio, of course Lucky *was* there. I was frightened, but Stephen played the whole thing as a huge joke.

'That's him over there, do you see? What d'you reckon our chances are?'

Alfred's wife looked cautiously over, but nothing happened. Lucky didn't move all evening, and when we got up to leave, he didn't stir. I knew though, that he had watched every movement, seen every gesture.

Time passed, of course, and I relaxed about Lucky. One reason was that Mandy, after a row with Peter, was sharing a flat with me in Dophin Square, Pimlico. Mandy didn't stay long; she patched up her relationship with Peter and went back to her old flat; but I stayed on, and spent a lot of time with Paul Mann, an old friend of Stephen's. We entertained a lot, held gambling parties, playing for fifty-pound stakes, and generally had a lot of fun, though we never had an affair. I felt that I had grown up and was in charge of my life. I thought I had forgotten about Lucky, and I hoped that he might have forgotten about me.

One night, sitting round the flat smoking pot, by then the 'in' thing amongst the Chelsea set, we decided to go to the All Nighter, the only late-night, loud music spot. There weren't any disco's in London yet.

As soon as we walked in, I saw Lucky. He came up to me and hung around our crowd. We tried to avoid him. Everyone had guessed who he was, but he wouldn't go away. He just wanted Paul and me to know that bygones were bygones, and that he wouldn't cause any more trouble. He was so persuasive that we believed him, and to show goodwill we invited him back to the flat. Looking back, I can hardly believe we did. It was one of the most thoughtless things I have ever done, and I have done a few.

We had decided to make a party of it, and when we got back to the flat, everyone was there. Paul put on a Johnny Mathis record. I was sitting on the sofa, watching Lucky as he went out of the door. Moments later he was back with an axe, one of the previous tenants had left behind. Everyone watched as he came towards me, and sat down on the sofa, putting the axe beside him.

Johnny Mathis sang on as everyone, except one of my girl friends, disappeared. They just got out of that flat as fast as they could. No one bothered to wait and see what was going to happen. Not one man stayed to protect us. As the room cleared, Lucky jumped up and locked the front door. Then he pulled me off the sofa and dragged me to the bedroom, brandishing the axe, his eyes blazing.

'I'll kill you this time! Kill, kill, kill!' He screamed, waving the axe round his head.

'Get your clothes off.'

'No you won't,' I thought, tearing my clothes off. Once his passion was spent, there was more chance of controlling him. There was no sound from my girl friend. In a second he had hurled the axe towards me. It sliced through the air, just missing my head. A second swipe knocked me practically senseless back onto the bed.

'For God's sake, get on with it.' I thought. But he hadn't yet made up his mind how to take me. He wanted me subjected and terrified into being gentle with him. He wanted sweetness, but I wasn't ready yet. I was getting used to this treatment.

The telephone rang.

'Answer it,' he ordered. 'And act like I'm not here. If you say anything . . .' He swung the axe round threatening.

It was a friend wanting to come round for a drink. I pretended I was tired and going to bed.

Lucky kept us in the flat for two days, wielding the axe to get his way. He never let up punching and slapping me until I was bruised and covered in fiery red sores. I cooked the meals while Lucky watched over us. He never let either of us out of his sight. When he took me into the bedroom, he left the door open, so he could keep an eye on my friend.

Smarting with pain, I realised I was going to have to make up to him, pretend that I liked him, if we were to get out alive. There was no way of communicating what I was doing to my friend, and she clearly thought I was off my head when I started, gradually, softening towards him. I got the strength to go through with it from knowing that only this way might we get a chance to escape.

As I became more pliable, Lucky relaxed. He still slept with the axe in his hand, but he had become a bit more pleasant to be with. In any other situation, you could have said he was good company.

Towards the end of the second day we ran out of food.

'Someone will have to go and get some, or we'll starve. There's a shop round the corner.' I told him.

'She can go.'

'She'll call for the police.' I explained simply, as you might to a child.

'You'll have to go, Lucky. I'll give you the keys.'

It was extraordinary, but he believed me. We'd run out of cigarettes, so he was keen to be off. As soon as he had gone, I rang the police. They rushed round and were ready for Lucky when he got back. There was no messing about. This time the evidence was there in black and blue, and

Lucky was charged with grievous bodily harm and taken into custody.

I wondered how long he would get, and what state he would be in when he got out. That's the worst thing about putting someone inside. The police hadn't been gone long, when Lucky's brother rang. He pleaded with me.

'We've all been trying to get Lucky to go straight. Look, don't charge him this time. I promise we'll keep him away from you.'

'It's too late, the police have already taken him away.'

'Listen, you got to drop those charges. He's my brother, see. And he's coloured. The police will have him in for a long time. They'll have no mercy. You drop the charges and I promise you won't see him again.'

'I'll ring you back. Give me your number.'

I wasn't sure what to do. I was dreading the thought of confronting Lucky in court. I would rather never see him again than have to go to court. The whole thing would be out. My parents would find out all about it. The press might get hold of it, who knew what? I decided it was better to let the whole business die out quietly. I rang the police and said I was going to drop the charges. They weren't at all happy about that, and insisted on coming round to talk about it first.

'Don't you understand he's a very dangerous character? He has a string of convictions behind him. Assault, larceny, even attempted murder. You were lucky this time, Miss Keeler, next time you might not get off so lightly.'

I was adamant.

'No. I'm dropping the charges.'

'Well we would rather you didn't.'

Why? I wondered. What was it to them?

'I'm perfectly entitled to drop them, aren't I?'

'Yes, miss. But we strongly advise that you don't.'

When they realised there was no persuading me they got angry, but that made no difference. So, having had their say, they left.

It was another very bad mistake. The next day Lucky Gordon was lurking round at Dolphin Square, leaning up against the wall, watching and waiting. In those days, I believed people when they told me they were going to do something. There was plenty more for me to go through before that was knocked out of me.

With Lucky in Dolphin Square, it was time for me to leave. I packed my bags and returned to the only person who understood: Stephen. He took me in, and I noticed that he had changed in my absence. He was exploring ever further afield to satisfy his erotic fantasies. He often drove round Paddington late at night, on his own. Sometimes he brought a prostitute back with him. He just wanted to see them walking round in his flat in their high heels and black stockings. The first one stole my underwear from the bathroom, and the second took my dance costume from the wardrobe. After that I kept my door locked.

There was a brief respite, but soon Lucky caught up with me. I had taken the precaution of putting on a strange voice when I answered the 'phone, but he saw through that. I just couldn't relax, knowing that wherever I went, I was being followed. Every time I left the flat, Lucky would be there, lurking. Then there would be a couple of weeks when I wouldn't see him. I began to breathe freely, thinking maybe he'd given up. Then there he was again, for no particular reason.

The fear became unbearable. The worst of it was not knowing when he might strike. It was driving me slowly mad. Gradually his obsession became mine. I found myself thinking about him day and night, trying to understand him. Thoughts rushed through my head, mad ideas. It was almost pervertedly flattering to arouse so much attention, to be in someone's mind every hour of the day. Yet I was scared. Scared to answer the 'phone, or walk out of the front door.

I think it was the feeling of total imprisonment that made me do what I did next. I had to confront my fears, meet them head on. The only way left was to seek out Lucky and I knew how to do that. I went to the club, alone.

I was quite unafraid that afternoon. Who was this, anyway, who had the right to make my life a misery? I didn't know what I was going to do when I saw him, I hadn't even worked that out. I only knew that if I enraged him, he would try and kill me. But that afternoon, I couldn't have cared less.

As soon as I entered the club and saw him standing there, my fears rushed over me. I would have run straight out again, if he hadn't already seen me. He walked over, took my arm and ordered me a cup of coffee.

I started talking. Gently, I told him that I couldn't carry on living in the same town as him if he was going to carry on pursuing me.

'Hey, don't you understand, Christine? I love you.'

I was silent.

'It's only 'cos I love you. I can't help it. It would be different if I wasn't black. That's all you've got against me, that so?'

I didn't have an answer.

'You must understand that I love you. That's all. I don't mean any bad for you. I just love you. I can't go away. It's better I see you at a distance, than nothing. But you won't give yourself the chance to love me. That's it, isn't it? You're afraid all the time about what people will say.'

He was still holding my arm fast.

'Have you never loved?'

'Of course I've been in love.'

'Then you know how I feel,' he said, putting his other hand to his heart.

I felt sorry for him. He might be wild, but he obviously did love me. I did mind what people would think, my mum in particular, about me seeing a black man. I would have lost my friends. Stephen would have drifted off, and everywhere I went, people would have whispered. It was different in those days. A white girl walking with a coloured man was something to stare at. No one had ever told me that it didn't matter what people thought of you, only what you thought about them.

'OK. If I see you occasionally, do you promise you won't try anything again, like last time?'

Lucky was so delighted, he was almost crying.

'We'll go to my brother's. They've got a house. You can stay for the day. Even a few days.'

'Only if you promise you won't try and scare me. I can't carry on, not knowing whether you're going to suddenly start behaving as though you're out to kill me.'

'I love you, Christine. Of course I won't hurt you. I only got mad because you wouldn't see me 'cos I'm black. Now you've come to me, everything's different.

It *was* very different. Lucky laughed and chatted as we drove to Leytonstone in a mini-cab. He kept pointing out where we were going and told me all about his brother's family. He told me how long he had lived with them, how long he had been staying there, how well his sister-in-law cooked and how pleased they would all be to see me.

When we arrived we went straight up to Lucky's room. It was sparsely furnished. There was a single bed, a chair and a chest of drawers with a television on top, plus Lucky's sister-in-law's washing, which hung off a clothes-horse in the middle of the room.

120

Lucky was a different person. He smiled instead of snarling, and his eyes were brown and gentle. Those hands which had scratched at my throat, now tenderly washed me with a flannel dipped in a basin of hot soapy water. I wasn't allowed to do a thing for myself. He brushed my hair and brought meals up from the kitchen.

We stayed together in that room for three days and all that time Lucky waited on me as though I were a princess. It was certainly a novel experience, and quite exciting. I put the axe-wielding brute who had savaged me out of my mind, and even began to believe that I could be happy with him. His love was so persuasive. He was totally content making love to me and talking about plans for our future.

But after three days the novelty wore off. I wanted to go out, buy my own cigarettes again, chat to Mandy and see Stephen. I didn't have the heart to tell him that things could never work out for the two of us, so I left telling Lucky that I'd see him again. He was so relaxed that he let me go without a fuss.

I went straight round to Stephen's, but I didn't want to stay long, because I knew Lucky would be on the 'phone. Back at Stephen's in my own familiar world, I realised too late that far from easing the situation I had only made matters worse. Why it didn't dawn on me before, I don't know. I can only put it down to the nervous state I had been driven to. I was too scared to think straight, and now I knew I had really blown it. If there had been trouble before, there was certainly going to be more when I didn't go back to Lucky.

Sure enough, the 'phone rang. It rang all afternoon but I left it ringing. When Stephen got back, he picked it up and of course it was Lucky.

'I'm not in,' I mouthed, frantically waving my arms.

Stephen hung up.

'Where the hell have you been? I've had your mother worrying herself to death. I had to lie and say you were with friends in the country, but hadn't left me the number. Where were you, why didn't you 'phone?'

'I couldn't. There wasn't a 'phone,' I said meekly.

'But where have you been?'

I told him the story.

'You're mad. Don't you realise the guy's a maniac? He could have killed you!'

'Don't be silly, Stephen. It wasn't a bit like that. He was very gentle. Do you know, he wouldn't even let me wash myself?'

'What?'

'Honestly. He waited on me. Did everything for me. Even washed me.'

'Washed you all over?'

'Yes, it was fun, really.'

'Well, really, Christine! You *are* a naughty little baby. Whatever will you do next?'

'I don't think I'd better stay here tonight. I'm sure Lucky will be round here looking for me. I'll go over to Michael's. I've spoken to him, and he's coming round to fetch me.'

Stephen was a bit annoyed at that. But he could see the sense in it, and at least it stopped him being cross with me for having disappeared like that.

11

AMERICA

MANDY RANG. She was fed up with England and had decided
to go to America for good with her old friend Nina Gadd.

'You've got to come, Christine. There's nothing going
on here. It's all happening over there.'

'I haven't got any money.'

'Well, come round and talk about it. We'll work out a
way for you to get some.'

The only time Mandy and I had been abroad together
was that disastrous trip to France. Nevertheless, I went
round to Mandy's flat. Nina was there, and we decided to
leave for the States in two weeks. The plan was for me to
stay on with Michael, hoping to persuade him to pay for
my trip. Nina, meanwhile, would stay with Stephen until
we were ready to leave, and Stephen didn't mind as she
offered to pay him five pound a week for rent.

There was no point in beating around the bush with
Michael – he knew me too well for that – so I came
straight to the point:

'Michael, I've been talking to Mandy and Nina and they
went me to go to the States with them in a fortnight. But I
need five hundred pounds to go.'

'*What?* You must be joking. You don't expect me to be
a party to that, do you?'

'I'm serious, Michael. If you don't lend it to me, I shall
go and get it somewhere else.'

'You most certainly will. I've already lent you money before, and I know what that means.'

'When?'

'For the flat.'

'You wanted me to go to the flat.'

'So that I could see you.'

'Well it wasn't my fault if you didn't. You could have done.'

'But every time I tried, you just happened to be busy. No, Christine. I am not going to "lend" you five hundred pounds, or for that matter five pounds, to go tripping off to America.'

'Then I shall just have to get it from somewhere else,' I threatened, and marched out of the room.

I liked the thought of Michael sitting there feeling jealous at the prospect. I was actually very fond of Michael. He didn't know very much about me, or about Lucky Gordon, nor did he see much of Stephen's or my friends, but I felt very safe with him. He had asked me to marry him, and I was seriously considering doing so.

I changed into a wonderfully sexy dress, and stalked back into the sitting-room.

'I'm off. See you later.'

One thing Michael did know was that I never threatened without intending to carry out the threat. Mind you, I would never have made that threat, if I hadn't known that Michael would soften. It wasn't as though he couldn't afford it.

'All right. But you will come back to me?'

'Of course I will,' I said, and I meant it.

Over the next few days I had such a lovely time with Michael I decided to stay in England. I really didn't want to leave him. He was one of the few men I really respected. He never stood for any nonsense from women, and at the same time he didn't throw his weight around trying to be macho.

So I rang Mandy to say I wasn't coming. She was terribly upset. Soon after I put the 'phone down, Nina rang to apologise, but she had just given my number to Lucky Gordon, not realising who he was. I was furiously miserable. That had ruined everything. Now I had no option but to escape to the States: anything was better than that Michael should get caught up in this Lucky business.

In the end, all turned out well. Michael's company needed a representative to go out to the States and Michael decided to go himself. So we spent the next few days in a whirl of injections and packing.

Mandy and I travelled together. The others were following later. The five days on the boat were tremendous fun, more fun than America turned out to be. As always we had an exciting time together, leading each other on. I bedded the captain and the senior officer, amongst others. As soon as we landed, we rushed off to see whether the New York clubs were better than the ones in London. It was all fantastic and I really thought this was *the* place to be. It was a new beginning. Lucky Gordon was just a part of my past, and fading fast. That moment of euphoria didn't last long.

It was very hot in New York, far hotter than anywhere I had ever been. We decided to visit Fire Island, a homosexual haunt. We arrived on the ferry to find no room at the hotel and no transport. Luckily we palled up with two men and shared their room. But I was terrified all night that Mandy's mink would be stolen, because I had heard all these stories about American crooks.

It wasn't, and the next morning we moved on to Cherry Grove and checked into a hotel at three in the afternoon.

We lay on the beach and sunbathed, shrieking with laughter at all the homosexuals who were having a lovely time displaying themselves. The only two men who weren't were the policemen. We made a date with them, but when they arrived we were so sunburnt that all they could do was rub our backs with lotion.

Nina never arrived. She stayed on at Stephen's flat. Michael wasn't due for three weeks, and of course Mandy and I ran out of money. Mandy decided she wanted to go back to Peter Rachman. I didn't know what to do.

'But I've got to stay, Mandy. Michael's coming out soon and we'll have great fun then.'

'Well, I'm not staying. You'll have to stay by yourself. I'm going back on the first available plane.' She had really made up her mind about it, and even booked her ticket, so I decided that somehow I would have to get the money and go back with her. I wasn't staying out on my own, it wasn't the kind of place you could do that.

I cabled Michael, reversing the charges, and asked him to wire me some more money, so that I could get home. I couldn't have borne three weeks in New York on my own, and when I spoke to Michael, I was nearly in tears, which is rare for me. I never let people know when I'm upset.

Flying is not one of my favourite means of travel. Usually I am convinced the 'plane's going to crash and we'll all be killed. I have to check that the wings and runway are all right. The sight of a loose rivet scares me rigid. If there's a bump, I think the engines have failed, and if I look out of the window I'm sick.

I drank a bottle of scotch before take-off, and had to be helped onto the 'plane and lain across three seats. Imagine my terror when I woke up to find the pilot standing talking to the passengers.

'What? You can't be the pilot,' I insisted.

'Yes, I am.'

'What on earth are you doing here? Whose flying the 'plane? You should get back immediately, otherwise we'll crash.' I was furious and wouldn't listen to his reasoning.

Touching down at London Airport was one of the happiest moments in my life – I could hardly believe we had arrived in one piece. The whole concept of flying totally defeats me. I might feel different if I could fly a plane myself, but as it is, I just don't trust pilots or 'planes. The whole idea of zooming around in the sky is totally unnatural.

I went straight to Michael's flat. He wasn't terribly pleased that I'd spoiled our plans. I tried to explain what a frightening place New York was on your own, and in the end he understood and forgave me for not waiting. We stayed together but there were problems. We were only happy when we were on our own. If we went out with friends, Michael was terribly possessive and jealous if I talked to anyone else, man or woman. When the time came for Michael to go to New York, I decided I wasn't going with him, and I moved back to Stephen's. There was nowhere else to go.

It was nearing the end of October and the Cuban Missile Crisis was looming. Stephen wanted to take a hand in trying to cement East/West relations. He went as far as getting his friend Lord Astor to write to the Foreign Office saying that if there was any way in which his friendship with Eugene Ivanov could be of use, in providing information about Russian intentions, Stephen would be delighted to help.

As a result of that letter, the Foreign Office gave Stephen an interview, but decided that he wasn't much use to them. Not only was he too broadminded politically, but he was inclined to talk too much. Furious at the rebuff,

Stephen got in touch with one of his old patients, Sir Godfrey Nicholson, a Conservative MP, and Chairman of the Parliamentary Estimates Committee.

President Kennedy announced a naval blockade of Cuba and told the Russians that any move on their part would be immediately retaliated in kind. It really did seem as if the world was on the brink of War.

Sir Godfrey wrote to the Foreign Secretary and got approval to meet Eugene Ivanov at Stephen's flat. I knew very little about those meetings. I gathered that it concerned holding a Summit Conference in London. This, it transpires, was Ivanov's proposal, clearly directed by Moscow, and its principal aim, as Harold Macmillan saw it, was to drive a wedge between America and Britain. Russia would have been glad if Britain had intervened. It would have given Russia more time to work out how they were going to get out of it all without losing face.

I stayed in my room during that meeting, but after the others had gone Stephen was terribly excited and jabbered on about underwater cameras being laid in the English Channel – something I have never subsequently figured out. Sir Godfrey also arranged for Stephen to meet the Permanent Under Secretary of State for lunch, but as far as I knew nothing came of it. There was so much going on that week, Stephen was in a constant flurry of meetings that we rarely had a chance to talk, and anyway much of what I heard meant little to me.

When news came that the Russian ships had turned back, Eugene was furious. I heard him arguing with Stephen long into the night and kept well out of the way, though I don't suppose they would have noticed me anyway, they were far too engrossed. By the time the crisis had blown over, Stephen, or any part he might have played, had been forgotten.

128

12

JOHNNIE

LIVING A few doors away from Stephen's consulting room in Devonshire Street was Paula Hamilton-Marshall, a prostitute Stephen used to visit sometimes. He took me along for coffee one day to her dull but spacious flat, where she lived with her younger brother John, a waiter. Paula looked after him because their mother had disowned them both.

Paula was pregnant by an American boyfriend who had left for his home country. It was at Paula's that I met another West Indian, Johnnie Edgecombe, who didn't have a regular job, but seemed better educated and more intelligent than Lucky Gordon. Paula knew quite a few West Indians through one of her former boyfriends. Naturally, Stephen and I told Johnnie all about Lucky.

'I only wish I had a gun to protect myself with – if I did I'd have no doubts about shooting him on sight.'

It was fear, not anger that provoked me to say that. Paula said she knew where I would be able to get a gun, and I decided I *was* going to get one. When I got to this place Paula told me about, I was surprised to be served by a respectable-looking Englishman, who seemed quite happy to sell it to me. I bought the gun and kept it in my handbag. It was just Lucky's luck that I never had it with me when he attacked.

It was impossible to stay at Stephen's for long. Lucky

knew I was there. So I moved into a flat with a friend called Kim Proctor. I had become friendly with Johnnie Edgecome, he came to stay with us, and while he was there conversation inevitably centred around Lucky.

One day as I came out of the hairdresser's with an American girlfriend I had met through Paula – it was near my old flat in Comeragh Road – Lucky pounced. I can only assume he found out where I was through one of Paula's crowd. He punched me to the ground without any warning. The American girl screamed and several people – there were plenty around – went to ring the police.

'This time I'm definitely prosecuting. It's only a pity that I didn't have my gun, or he wouldn't be alive now.'

'Oh, Christine, please don't,' said the girl. 'I haven't got a permit to stay in England. I'll be in real trouble. They'll send me back to the States.'

What could I do? I just jumped in the first cab and rushed straight round to Kim's. Johnnie was there, and when he saw my bruises and heard the full story, he decided to deal with Lucky himself. Perhaps this was the answer, one West Indian against another.

Johnnie called Lucky and they had a long argument. He told Lucky where we were, and Lucky came round to have it out. Johnnie went downstairs to face him. I stood six feet from the door of our flat, and stood there pointing the gun. Kim was hysterical so I told her to go and sit down.

'Don't worry, Kim. If Lucky walks through that door, I'll kill him.'

I waited, arm stretched out. Then Johnnie came back upstairs. Lucky had run off.

That night I went back to Stephen. Kim went to stay with Paula, and Johnnie moved into a hotel in Kensington Close.

130

A few weeks later, on 27th October, Johnnie and I went to the All Nighter. Lucky was there as usual, smoking and drinking with his mates. As soon as Johnnie and I appeared, Lucky rushed over and grabbed a chair to hit Johnnie with. Johnnie lost his temper as Lucky chased me through the club. Johnnie in turn gave chase and I managed to lose myself amongst the people on the dance-floor. Whilst he was searching for me, Johnnie caught up with Lucky. A couple of girls were screaming while the men stood back silently, watching and waiting to see what would happen next.

Lucky made a rush for the exit with Johnnie close behind, but the bouncers were in the way. Johnnie came towards him and as I got nearer, I saw Johnnie pull out a knife. He slashed Lucky's face, causing blood to spurt everywhere. I looked away, sickened.

Lucky screamed with rage and pain. The cut ran from his forehead to his chin down the side of his face, and the blood poured into his eyes, blinding him.

'You'll go inside for this!' he screamed. 'I'll get the law, you'll go inside.'

Johnnie grabbed my arm.

'Come on! You're coming with me,' he ordered, pulling me towards the door.

'He'll get the police on to me – and his brothers,' said Johnnie, back at his hotel room. He was throwing his clothes into a case. He had decided to get out of town and was taking me with him. I didn't argue, even though I had been shocked by the knife. I didn't realise that Johnnie had taken it with him.

I rang Stephen and told him what had happened, and that Johnnie wouldn't let me go. Stephen came round right away to reason with him, but Johnnie wasn't listening. As far as he was concerned, the best thing for me was to get out of town with him. Stephen left after I assured him I would be back in a couple of days. With my gun jammed in my handbag, Johnnie and I grabbed a taxi and drove to Brentwood.

13

SHOTS

AFTER A couple of days in Brentwood, I went round to tell Stephen about the slashing at the All Nighter, and at the flat I met an acquaintance of his called Michael Eddowes, who invited me out for dinner at one of his restaurants – he owned the El Bistro chain as well as being a solicitor, and he had written a book called *The Man on Your Conscience* about the trial of Timothy Evans and the murders at 10 Rillington Place: a tall, impressive man in his fifties, this was someone I would indeed meet again.

Meanwhile, I was still out at Brentwood, but my stay came to an abrupt end when Stephen rang and told me to come round immediately if I was interested in getting a new flat. Leaving Johnnie was now going to be a problem. I tried to act as normally as possible and looked around casually for my gun, which he had hidden from me. I couldn't spot it, so I just pretended I was off for the day and kissed him goodbye, my heart in my mouth.

When I arrived at Stephen's flat, I noticed that there were a lot of suitcases piled up in the hall: they belonged to a girl called Rosemary, the daughter of one of Stephen's friends. Then Stephen told me that Lucky had been round to the flat and had dramatically pressed some little black things, like insects, into Stephen's hand. They were the stitches from Lucky's face.

'Give them to her. She'll be needing them.'

Stephen tried to make light of the situation with Lucky and Johnny, saying to me: 'You should arrange to meet both of them together under the same clock!'

I was too upset to laugh. In the sitting-room Eugene Ivanov was chatting with William Shepherd, a Tory MP who used to hang out at Murray's occasionally. Eugene was also upset, but about more international matters than a handful of stitches: he felt that his country had been humiliated over Cuba, and Stephen was animated too. After Shepherd had gone, they left together for a party at Iain Macleod's – at that time he was Chairman of the Conservative Party – but they returned in some confusion over the arrangements. It seemed like high-flying stuff, but it was nothing to do with me, and later that night Rosemary and I moved into a flat just around the corner from Devonshire Mews. Things then started to look up. Stephen helped me to get my modelling started again, and through his connections lined me up with a string of jobs.

Then we heard that Peter Rachman had died suddenly of a heart attack. Mandy was in France. She returned to hear the news from Stephen, and she was distraught at Peter's death. She cried and cried, not knowing what she was going to do, how she would get by.

Mandy moved back in with Stephen, and soon started to carry on with a man called Emil Savundra, destined to become known as 'the Indian Doctor' in court, and later even more famous under his own name for one of the biggest frauds of the '60s. Mandy certainly could pick them. Savundra had been paying Stephen £25 a week for the use of the flat when he wanted somewhere to take his girlfriends during the day. Now a dreadful row broke out between Mandy and Stephen, because he had been going round telling everyone that Mandy's first remark on hearing of Peter's death had been:

'Did he leave a will?'

It turned out that he had been telling a few tales about me too. I dropped round to see Mandy at Stephen's flat when he was out. She hadn't been out of bed for ages – she really was terribly depressed. I made some coffee in the kitchen, and when I came back I discovered that she had swallowed a bottle of aspirin. I rang for an ambulance, which rushed her off to hospital where they were able to treat her. She was well again in no time, but still refused to get on with her life.

'Oh, come on,' I said, trying to sound enthusiastic, 'Let's go shopping.'

'I can't.'

'Well, it's no good you lying there. There are plenty of other people in the world. So you might as well get up and start enjoying yourself again.'

She started dressing herself, very slowly and lazily, but at least she had agreed to get up and put on some makeup and go shopping. The telephone rang twice. I hadn't answered it since I'd been back in London, fearing it might be Lucky, but for some reason, this time I did. It was Johnnie Edgecombe.

'Look, I'm not living here at Stephen's, Johnnie. I'm just visiting Mandy, and anyway I told you not to ring my friends.' I was angry with him, because I really hoped I had got all that business behind me.

'Can I see you for a minute, please?'

'No, you can't.' I replied roughly and slammed the 'phone down. It was too much to bear. First one and now the other.

'I'll come out if you do one thing for me. Please, Christine,' said Mandy.

'What is it?'

'Ring Peter's wife and find out if *she* knows whether he left me anything.' (He hadn't.)

'No, I can't, Mandy,' I was firm. 'I rang her when you wanted her to know you had tried to commit suicide. What's the point?'

'Everyone thinks I'm not upset about Peter but I am, and I can't go on with Stephen telling everyone and being horrid. It's dreadful enough without Peter. Stephen only makes it worse.'

'Well, don't be silly. Come out and do some shopping. You'll feel much better.'

At last Mandy was ready, except for her hair; she spent another ten minutes doing that.

'Come on. For heaven's sake, hurry up!'

The doorbell rang. Mandy looked out of the window as I was about to answer it.

'It's Johnnie.'

He had come straight round in a mini-cab. I was terrified.

'Are you going to let him in?'

'No. Tell him I'm at the hairdresser's.'

Mandy leaned out of the window.

'She's gone to the hairdresser's.' She yelled, not very convincingly.

'I want to come in.'

'But she's not here. She left a few minutes ago.'

'I'm going to come in.'

Mandy looked at me.

'Tell him I'm not here.'

'She's not here.'

'I just want to talk to her. Let me in so I can see her.'

I decided to go to the window.

'What do you want, Johnnie?'

'Come down to the door. I can't speak to you from here.'

'Say what you have to from there.'

'Just come down, please,' he pleaded. He looked rather pale and ill.

'Have you got the gun on you?'

He shook his head and felt his pockets. I didn't believe him.

'If you don't go, I shall have to ring the police.'

I went to the 'phone and dialled 999. While I was waiting for a reply, Johnnie fired his first shot at the house. I dropped the 'phone and rushed to the window.

'Johnnie! What are you doing? You'll get into terrible trouble. You must go.'

He heard me and aimed straight at me. I dived down and waited. Then slowly I raised my head to see if he was still down below. He had been waiting for me and took another shot. He missed, but before he took another shot I rushed downstairs to make sure that the garage door was closed.

As I ran back upstairs, Johnnie started shooting at the lock on the front door. Mandy had finished on the 'phone.

'The police are coming,' she gasped from the floor, where she was trying to wriggle under the bed.

'You're not going under there. What if Johnnie breaks open the door? He's shooting at the lock, you know. Come on! We'll go near the window. We'll have a better chance that way.'

We stood on either side of the room, giggling and waiting for something to happen. There was silence. I peered out of the window. Johnnie's mini-cab driver was still waiting outside, but there was no sign of Johnnie. The next time I looked the cab had gone.

The police had arrived soon afterwards and searched the house and garden. They examined the bullet-holes and found the gun hidden in the drawer of an old table in the garden. Meanwhile, I rang Stephen.

'Get Mandy out at once. I'm not coming back to the house until she's gone.'

'We've got to go the police station now.'

'Then make sure you take her back to your place. I don't want to be involved in any of this.'

'It's bloody mean of him,' Mandy whined. 'He's just a mean, vicious old man. I'm fed up with him, I'll be glad if I never see him again.'

One lot of policemen were sent off to Brentwood to pick up Johnnie. The others took Mandy and me down to the station. In no time at all, reporters had gathered as if from nowhere outside the station to interview and photograph us.

The police kept us waiting a long time with question after question. They already knew all about Lucky Gordon and, while I was in the station, Johnnie was picked up at Brentwood. I had given the police his address. This time there was no doubt at all. I would have to appear in court. During the time I was answering all the questions fired at me about the slashing incident at the All Nighter and the shooting, they never once asked whose gun it was. So I didn't tell them.

I was trying to work out a way of keeping myself *out* of the news, or at least to make certain that if I did go to court, I wouldn't have to give personal details of my relationship with Johnnie. I was terrified that my mother would find out that I had coloured friends. She would have been mortified.

The police told Mandy and I that we wouldn't be required to give evidence until after Christmas, which gave me a little time to work out how to avoid being asked the one question I was afraid of. The press had made the most of the shooting incident because it had happened at Stephen's flat, and he was well known in society as an artist who entertained a great many people with titles and other credits to their names.

Or was it more than that?

14

HAWKS

WE COLLECTED Mandy's clothes and she came to stay with me. It was nearly Christmas, and we had masses of things to sort out before the 25th. Every day we were bombarded with reporters who rang the door-bell or telephoned. Mandy was pleased with the publicity, but I was afraid. Johnnie was going to make it clear to the police and the press that I had been living with him in Brentwood. At all costs I wanted to avoid being asked in court:

'Did you have intercourse with the accused?'

I felt that I could not face my friends and relations ever again if that came out in public.

Rosemary soon left the flat. It was all too much trouble for her. Paul Mann, his old bridge-playing friend from the Connaught, was staying with Stephen, who thought it would be a good idea to have him there in the midst of all the publicity.

I was going to need a solicitor, but how was I going to pay him? I wasn't getting any work since the shooting – the publicity had destroyed that. I turned up one day to do a commercial I'd been booked for, only to have the producer bluntly announce that he couldn't use me because I was the girl in the West Indian shooting scandal.

Then I remembered Michael Eddowes. He was delighted when I rang him, and came round immediately.

'It looks as though Edgecombe will get a heavy sentence,'

he said. 'I suppose they'll tie up the slashing incident at the same time.'

'But can I have a solicitor or something, so that when I'm asked, "Did you sleep with him?', he can call out, "Objection"? The press have been so insistent. They're bound to make the most of it because he's black, and I just don't want it to come out in the papers that I had sex with him.'

'Look, Christine, the man will be fighting for his life, he is facing a very long sentence. He will tell the court he slashed Lucky to protect you and the details of that relationship will come out. Then they will want to know why a young girl living with an older man should need a gun, and how you acquired it. They might blame you for provoking both attacks and want to know how you came to be mixed up with such people in the first place.'

'Stephen is frightened of being mentioned. He doesn't want it to come out how we met.'

'I can appreciate that. But I'm sure all these questions can be avoided. There needn't be any scandal at all. Now you'd better tell me everything you can remember: who you've met, where and how, right from when you first came to London. Then we will have something to work on. It wouldn't be so good if the defence turned the tables and suggested you provoked the slashing – or, for that matter, the shooting.'

'I see,' I said, and meekly answered his questions.

Michael moved in some of the same circles as Stephen, and he knew about my affair with Profumo. Maybe the press had got to know something too, and that was why they were so interested in me now?

'How long ago was it that you last had anything to do with John Profumo?' Michael now asked.

I laughed.

'What can that possibly have to do with this? It was over a year and a half ago.'

'But it was about the time that you first met Lucky Gordon, wasn't it?'

'Yes, I suppose so.'

'Did John Profumo ever meet Lucky?'

'No, of course not.'

'You've said that Stephen introduced you to Lucky?'

'Well, he took me down to the club, yes.'

'Can you prove that?'

'Yes, of course. Vasco Lazzolo was there, and Stephen wanted a black girl. But this is nothing to do with the shooting. Why should they ask anything about all that?'

'Calm down, Christine.' Michael said kindly. 'Just tell me the things I have to know in order to help you, and I'm sure we'll be able to avoid anything getting out at all. Now how about Eugene Ivanov? Did you ever have anything to do with him?'

'Yes. Once.'

'How long ago?'

'About the same time that I knew Jack. But I don't understand how this makes any difference.'

'So you had an affair with them both at exactly the same time?'

'I don't see what it's got to do . . .' I began. But Michael explained.

'Remember, you met Lucky Gordon for the first time when you were having an affair with both Jack Profumo and Eugene Ivanov, the Russian.'

'I wasn't having an affair with both at the same time. I only ever had anything to do with Eugene once.'

'And about the questions you were asked.'

'What questions?'

'I remember you telling me something about Eugene

142

asking you to find out when the Americans were going to give the Germans the bomb.'

'No, that was Stephen. Not Eugene. He would never have done anything like that. It was Stephen joking.'

'You might have thought it was a joke. But it wasn't to him. You must tell the police about that one, Christine. It's important.'

'But it all happened ages ago. How can it be important now.'

'I don't expect you to understand international affairs, Christine, but I can assure you that you might be in a lot of trouble if you don't come clean about this.'

'Well, I don't understand, Michael. Honestly, I don't. All I want is for someone to prevent my being questioned about whether I slept with Johnnie Edgecombe.'

'I am sure we can work something out,' Michael assured me. 'I'll get in touch with you when I've found out what counts they are charging him with, and we'll see what we can do.'

He never telephoned me again.

Meanwhile, a rumour had got about that I was going to mention Profumo's name in court, and this reached Stephen in no time.

Stephen had lunch with Jack Profumo and Bill Astor the following day and he suggested to them that something ought to be done to shut me up for, as Stephen explained, nobody wanted to be involved in this sordid little drug and pistol affair. It could ruin their reputations. That afternoon Bill came to see me to find out whether I had any intentions of mentioning him.

'Of course your name doesn't come into it.'

'There's no need to worry about it, Christine. I will handle everything. I'll fix you up with a solicitor and barrister and pay for the costs.'

He seemed to treat the whole thing very lightly and I was greatly relieved.

Here at last, I thought, is a Lord who after all does know what things are about. And if he says everything will be OK, it will.

Having satisfied himself that he wouldn't be involved, Bill was all for jumping into bed with me. When I declined, he took Mandy instead.

Two days later neither Michael Eddowes nor Bill Astor had rung. My mother telephoned, however. Lucky Gordon had been round there!

The newspapers reporting the shooting incident had given out her address and Lucky turned up on the doorstep, demanding to see me.

'It was dreadful, Christine,' my mother cried down the telephone.

'A black man. And all the neighbours could see. I was so afraid, Chris, honest. I went through the back and climbed over the fence. I went next door and stayed there, but he didn't go away. He just sat on the hill opposite until it got dark. You've no idea how dreadful it was. I thought he was going to kill me!'

I reported it to the police, but there was nothing they could do. I was terribly upset and frightened, thinking that Lucky was *still* out looking for me. Since the police had been involved, I thought he had left me alone. The only people I now allowed in the flat were Kim, now my closest friend, Mandy, Nina Gadd and Paul Mann.

The following day, Paul and I were invited to a party given by an old friend, Sheila Dring, who I had known at the Cabaret Club. There I met John Lewis, a former Labour MP.

'Are you the girl in the shooting incident?'

'Yes.'

'I've just successfully sued the newspapers for a quarter of a million pounds, so I do know a little about legal proceedings. Maybe I could offer you some advice?'

I told him about the problem with Johnnie and Lucky.

'Give me your telephone number. I'll make an appointment for you to see my solicitor tomorrow morning,' he smiled kindly.

He looked a good-hearted soul. Quite humourous. A fat, balding chubby-chops. I didn't know that he was simply a power-struck little man intent on getting his own back on Stephen, who had been Joy Lewis' friend and testified on her behalf in the vitriolic Lewis divorce. And I certainly had no idea that Lewis had learned about me from Michael Eddowes. This insidious man was now sniffing round me to see what information he could glean that might indict Stephen.

I was pleased when John Lewis rang the next day and invited me to his house. At last some action! When I arrived, he asked the same kind of questions as Michael Eddowes, but seemed less inquisitive. He succeeded in gaining my confidence. He told me that Frank Sinatra and Ava Gardner had once stayed in his flat whilst he was away. It was a smart place. There was a large dining-cum-sitting room, a morning room where I was seen, an office and a very large kitchen.

'I keep dossiers on a great many people in there,' he told me, pointing to the office.

As I got to know him, he became more familiar with me and once made a pass. Our meetings usually ended in shouting matches as I insisted that my relations with John Profumo and Eugene Ivanov had nothing to do with the case against Johnnie Edgecombe.

'None of that can possibly come up.'

'It will. It will. If you don't admit it, you'll be put away for perjury,' he shouted. He frightened and convinced me completely. He wasn't rich and powerful for nothing. I believed that he understood my predicament, and he kept his promise and *did* introduce me to his solicitor, which was more than anyone else had done.

15

BETRAYAL

On New Year's Eve, Stephen rang and invited me to a party. I took Kim along. On the way back, Stephen was driving. Kim and I were squeezed into the front of the two-seater and Stephen's friend, Earl Fenton, was squashed in the back. Stephen was very irritable and started swerving dangerously.

'Slow down, Stephen. You're going too fast,' I said.

'Kim will have to get out and get a taxi,' he shouted. 'I can't drive properly.'

'Don't be silly, Stephen. 'It's snowing. She'll never find one.'

'I don't care,' he snapped.

I was so angry that I made him pull up, and Kim and I both got out of the car. I slammed the door behind. When we got back to our flat, Stephen rang. I was surprised after what had just happened.

'That damn Paul. He's a real bastard. He and his friend Jerry were having it off in my bedroom.'

He was furious. I didn't have the face to put the phone down.

'What did you do?'

'I've thrown them out and got my key back. They'll never stay here again!'

A few days later I saw Mandy. She was livid. Stephen had moved out of his flat to avoid the reporters and had moved into the flat where she had lived with Peter Rachman. Later on Kim turned up and told me that Stephen was telling everyone that I had introduced him to the delights of Paddington (not the other way round), and that I was dabbling in drugs.

I wondered what he had told the Inspector from the Narcotics Squad who had visited Stephen's flat when Lucky had attacked me there. Stephen had ordered me out of the room so that he could talk privately with the Inspector. Why had Stephen even called round the Narcotics Squad for a case of grievous bodily harm? It didn't make sense.

I decided to have it out with Stephen. I made Kim ring him and listened in on the extension.

'Hi! How are you getting on?' she asked. 'What's happened about the shooting and all that?'

'That silly girl. I'm really very angry with her. It's not very pleasant being mixed up in the whole business. West Indians, drugs. She's completely scatter-brained. To think I've done all I could to keep her out of trouble, all the way down the line. She has no consideration for other people at all.'

'That's lies, Stephen!' I interjected. 'And if they ask me where I met Lucky, I'm going to tell them, I promise you. I'll tell them all about how we met them and why. I'm going to tell the truth!'

Stephen slammed down the 'phone. Kim gave me a sympathetic but 'told you so' look. But what was that compared to a broken friendship? I just couldn't believe it. After so many years of companionship. One telephone call, one betrayal. It totally changed my attitude to Stephen.

Mandy hadn't had her say yet.

'Well, he's not getting away with using my flat. I'm going to ring and tell him.'

She did.

'You're using my blankets and my fridge and my furniture and heaters. It's my electricity bill, and all the things in that flat are mine!'

'Yours!' Stephen laughed. 'Without Peter you would have had nothing. NOTHING.'

'And because Peter's dead you think you can take everything, I suppose. Well, you can't, Stephen. I've got receipts for some of those things and I'll take you to court if you try.'

'Oh, can't I? I'm certain you wouldn't stand a chance. I'm sure Peter's wife won't object to my being here. It's her flat, by rights, you know.'

'You can't get away with it.'

'We'll see about that, Mandy,' he said and hung up.

The solicitor that John Lewis had recommended listened to my fears that I would have to testify to having had a relationship with Johnnie Edgecombe.

'It's useless to summon a barrister. Questions about your past cannot be avoided. But we'll do our best for you.'

Again I told John Lewis what had happened. I was beginning to feel that everyone who had promised help was only trying to use me in some way. John started to question me again and again about my relations with John Profumo, Eugene Ivanov and 'Mr Woods'. I discovered too late that he had been recording our conversation. By this time he had contacted the Labour MP George Wigg and was trying to persuade him to investigate Profumo. The tape recording was more ammunition for Wigg.

When he left the office, I locked him out. So you've got a dossier on Stephen, I thought. Let's see what it says. And I wonder if there's one on me too? I didn't find much and was too scared to tear anything up, though it was

149

tempting. Soon he was back and banging on the door. I refused to let him in, but then he fetched his housekeeper. I felt a bit ridiculous with her standing out there, so I gave in.

On another occasion, John Lewis offered me a large sum of money if I would sleep with him. Perhaps he wanted to tape that too, in which case it might have come in very useful later when they tried to get Stephen. I refused. He resorted to calling me names, telling me I was an alcoholic and a whore. That I'd never have another opportunity to make any money, that my future was ruined.

- 'I'm not going to let you go until you make love to me,' he shouted.

'That's what you think,' I said calmly, making for the door. He punched me aside and pompously repeated his demand.

'You'll have to shoot me before you go,' he said, walking out of the room and locking the door. He returned with a gun and gave it to me.

'If you won't make love to me, you'll have to shoot me if you want to leave. It's loaded. Go ahead.'

'Don't be silly. I *will* shoot if you don't let me go.'

He still barred my way. I pulled the trigger. The gun wasn't loaded. I will never forget the face of that man when he heard the click of the trigger.

'You would have shot me!' he stammered. 'You would have done it!'

I left. At least *that* little game was over.

* * * * *

The reporters had been sitting on my doorstep for a month waiting for me to talk to them. I still didn't really understand what all the fuss was about. Paul Mann, Mandy and Nina did. Nina turned up one day with a man she said was her fiancé. I let them in, and Nina began the conversation:

'You used to know John Profumo, didn't you, Christine?'

'Yes, so what?'

'People like that never seem to help you when you need it. Look, you've got barely anything to eat and a West Indian is after your blood. The best thing you could do would be to sell your story about Profumo to one of the papers, then get out of the country until things die down.'

'Yes, why don't you?' Mandy added. 'All those reporters have been trying to get hold of you. You should make use of the publicity. See what you can get out of it. It may be a long time before you can do any modelling again. You'd be a fool not to.'

Paul chipped in too.

'Have you got any proof?'

'I've got a letter from John Profumo.'

'That's all you need.'

'But I couldn't get him into trouble.'

'How could you? You know they can't print names. They'd be sued. So it would only be a story about how you knew a Russian agent and a Minister at the same time. That's all,' Nina's friend explained.

'How much d'you think they'd give me?'

I liked the idea of getting some money. After all, it wouldn't hurt Jack, and I needed the money to move again. Kim had told me she had seen Lucky outside the flat.

'You'd get about a thousand pounds. Maybe more.' Nina's friend said. 'I work for the *Sunday Pictorial*. Here's my card.' I thought there had been something fishy about him. And Nina, it turned out, was herself working as a freelance journalist.

151

I took the card and rang him the next morning, then went straight round to his office, taking Mandy with me.

'You the girl in the shooting?' the reporter asked.

'Yes, I haven't any money. My modelling career is finished, so I need the money. But I don't want to get anyone into trouble.' I said naïvely.

We discussed the story. 'My Life With a Minister.'

'Yes. One coming in the front door as the other one goes out of the back door.' Mandy giggled.

Everyone laughed. I showed them Jack's letter. The reporters said they'd take the story as long as I left the letter with them as evidence, in case it was needed. They agreed to give me two hundred pounds then, and eight hundred when I signed the proofs.

'We'll put it together for you. Then you come in and sign in about three weeks.'

Mandy and I left the office gaily.

Three days later Detective-Sergeant John Burrows, from Marylebone Police Station, came round to see us. He told us that evidence would be taken at the Magistrates' Court on the 16th of January. He seemed an honest and pleasant man. It was a change to have someone in the house whom I could trust and felt safe with. I felt I could put my faith in him and I desperately needed someone to confide in. I poured out my troubles over a cup of tea as he listened very sympathetically.

Both Mandy and I spoke badly of Stephen because of the way he had treated us. I had heard that Stephen had become a different person – bitter and old-womanish with everyone. He was no longer the laughing man I had known before. Once we had chased down the streets amongst the West Indians, our feet hardly touching the ground, but reality now hit him hard, and there were rumours that he was trying to get me silenced. Whispers spread fast. Stephen was afraid of something. The man whom I had always respected, who had taught me how to feel again, how to live, had denied and betrayed me. It hurt too deeply. I had understood when other friends of his had been dropped, but there had always been a place for me, his 'little baby'. I would accept his stern orders, laugh when he laughed, sympathise, be silent, be talkative, and live according to his rules.

Now John Burrows took his place as the man I could trust and confide in. He was a policeman and I had absolute faith in his profession. I believed that if I told him the truth, providing he liked me and knew me to be honest, everything would be all right. If only it had been that simple.

'I can't get in trouble because *he* attacked *me*, can I?'

The way everyone was talking, I had begun to think I was the one who was in trouble, not Johnnie.

'Of course not. You're only a witness. What's bothering you?'

'People say I enticed him. But it's not true. Stephen took me to the West Indian club in the first place.'

'Yes, it was Stephen's fault,' Mandy assured him.

Detective Burrows asked questions about Stephen's girlfriends, about the cottage and Cliveden.

'I should think he's had every girl in London,' said Mandy. 'It's all right for a time, but then he just drops you. It's the same with all of them. He threw me out and then took my flat, would you believe it? Now I have to live here. I had the flat Peter Rachman left me, and Stephen's taken everything in it.'

'Doesn't sound good, any of it. What does he get up to, apart from, . . . well?' he grinned.

'All that's happened is his fault,' Mandy added. 'He got her into trouble and now wants her to take the blame. He won't have anything to do with either of us now.'

'Lord Astor came to offer me a solicitor. John Lewis and Stephen's friend, Michael Eddowes, all said they would help, but they were only interested in my affair with John Profumo and the Russian. So in the end I just had to go to a newspaper and sell the story to pay for a solicitor.'

'What story was that?'

'About Jack and Ivanov. I haven't signed the proofs yet, but they gave me two hundreds pounds and I'll get another eight hundred when the proofs are ready,' I made some excuses:

'I haven't got Jack into trouble. They can't print his name, you see.'

'And what exactly was the story about?'

I told him all about the affair.

'And how did you come to know these people?'

'Stephen introduced me to them.'

I was living with him, so naturally I met his friends. Many of Stephen's girlfriends, including Bill Astor's wife, had met their husbands through Stephen. But that wasn't what Burrows thought.

In his report he claimed that I had said Doctor Ward was a procurer of women for gentlemen in high places, and that he was sexually perverted. He said Ward had a country cottage on Lord Astor's estate, where some of these women were invited to meet important men. That Ward had introduced me to John Profumo and that I had an association with him and that Profumo had written to me a number of letters on War Office notepaper, one of which I still possessed and which was being considered for publication in the *Sunday Pictorial*. He also reported that on one occasion, during the Berlin Wall Crisis, when I was going to meet Mr Profumo, Ward had asked me to discover from him the date on which certain atomic secrets were to be handed to West Germany by the Americans.

154

He also reported that Stephen had introduced me to the Russian Naval Attaché, Eugene Ivanov, and that I had met him on a number of occasions.

Burrows had pieced together our angry chatter to make a dynamic report. No doubt his superiors were impressed.

That same day Stephen learned that I had gone to the *Sunday Pictorial*. He immediately went to see his friend William Rees-Davies, a barrister, to try and stop publication. He also rang Bill Astor, who told Jack Profumo what was going on.

Jack sent his solicitor round to see me. He gave me the name of another solicitor who he suggested I should use to negotiate with him how much money I wanted not to publish the story. By now I realised that although I had been told that no names would be mentioned, I had obviously done something wrong. I didn't dare tell him that I had given John's letter to the *Sunday Pictorial*. I said I had destroyed all the letters.

When Paul Mann came round I told him about the solicitor's visit.

'I expect they'll try to buy you off. Can't you see they're worried? I think I had better handle this for you, Christine.'

'The solicitor left me a number and asked me to see them tomorrow. What shall I do?'

'I'll deal with it. You really should get your own solicitor. If you use someone they suggest you won't get as much money.'

I was uncertain, but Paul insisted that I found myself a solicitor. The man he took me to was Gerald Black, someone Stephen had recommended. Paul had been dividing his time between my flat and Stephen's, and no doubt he had an interest in cleaning up the mess.

While Paul waited outside Mr Black's office, I was advised not to sell my story.

'But I've already given it to the *Pictorial* and they've promised to put me up in a hotel to protect me from Lucky Gordon.'

'It could do a great deal of damage,' Mr Black explained gently. He began by treating me properly as his client, but as the afternoon wore on, it became apparent that he too was not acting on my behalf.

'How much are the newspapers paying you?'

'A thousand pounds.'

I told Mr Black that Paul had advised me that Profumo wanted to buy the story from me, and if so, I wanted five thousand pounds not to publish. With that I would be able to buy my mother a proper home, one that Lucky would never find.

I gave Mr Black the number of Jack's solicitor and finally left. The following day I rang him and was told that Mr Profumo had no intention of buying me off. The whole idea had been fabricated by Paul. Stephen's solicitor, Rees-Williams, with whom Black, a former pupil of his, had other business to discuss, had however agreed on Stephen's behalf to pay the five thousand.

I agreed too, and Mr Black collected fifty pounds that afternoon so that I could pay my hotel bill. He asked to collect the balance the next day. Paul seemed quite happy with the arrangement, so we put off the *Sunday Pictorial*, who kept ringing and asking me to go round and sign the proofs.

The following day at his office, Mr Black asked about the proofs.

'You haven't signed them yet, have you?'

'No, of course not.'

'I've got the money for you here, five hundred pounds. Well, four hundred and fifty to be precise, as we've already had fifty.'

156

'I don't understand. You agreed five thousand with the solicitor.

I was so confused by now that I hardly knew whose solicitor was whose. They were obviously all in it together. Before I had a chance to fly into a rage over that trick, he was telling me that there were conditions too.

'And what are they?'

'Firstly, you must break your friendship with Mandy . . .'

What on earth had Mandy done that warranted such venom from Stephen?

'And, you must arrange for your parents to be placed in a hotel until everything has blown over. Thirdly, as soon as the case is over, you must leave the country for a month. When you return,' he said with a twisted smile, 'everyone, I can assure you, will be on your side. They'll see you're OK for the future. But, if you don't agree . . .' he continued hurriedly, as I got up to leave, 'things will be very different for you. I suppose you noticed that girl sitting in the outer office?'

'Yes, why?' I had seen this frightful, skinny creature hunched up in the corner.

'She sold her story to the newspapers once, and look where it got her. Before, she had everything. Good looks, plenty of influential friends, but afterwards – naturally, no one wanted to know her.'

'How dare you! What are you suggesting? That I'll look like that one day? The conditions are ridiculous. My parents wouldn't live in a hotel for one minute. And as for me leaving the country for a month to let things quieten down . . . let me tell you, it was Stephen's so-called friends and acquaintances who started all the scandal in the first place – at my expense. Let them sort it out. You can tell them to keep their filthy money and cheap threats. I'm

157

going to sign the proofs. You can tell them I don't care. Tell them what you like!'

I stormed out of the office past the snivelling creature on the bench.

I went round to the *Sunday Pictorial*'s offices with Paul and signed the proofs. There was no mention of John Profumo by name.

'We'll let you have a cheque for the eight hundred when we're sure we can publish.'

'When will you know?' asked Paul.

'We'll ring and let you know tomorrow.'

Neither Paul nor I had heard that an application had been made to adjourn the trial because one of the witnesses – Johnnie's mini-cab driver – had been taken ill. In the event, the trial was postponed until March. Then the *Sunday Pictorial* rang to say that they had decided *not* to publish. They were going ahead with another story about me by Dr Ward.

16

SPAIN

EVERYONE WAS in a hurry to go. Mandy went to stay with Earl Fenton, while Kim and Paul wanted to go to Spain.

'Why don't you come with us, and get away from it all?' they suggested.

'What about the trial? Anyway, I haven't got the money.'

'Oh, don't worry about that. None of us has, but we'll manage somehow. Paul's got some insurance money he can pick up in Spain.'

'I can't not turn up, though.'

'Oh, let them get on with it,' Kim said. 'Let's get away from it all.'

'You haven't committed a crime,' Paul explained. 'You're only a witness against Johnnie. They can't do anything to you.'

'You'll have plenty of sunshine.'

'Sea, sand.'

'Wine.'

I wasn't persuaded by their arguments. But a more forceful one turned up in the form of Lucky Gordon, who had found out which hotel I was staying at. Kim, Paul and I escaped from the hotel in Paul's Jaguar, with Lucky in hot pursuit.

We drove straight out of London, crossed the Channel and didn't stop until we arrived, exhausted, at a little fishing village near Alicante. At a local café we asked for accommodation and found a villa for thirty shillings a week, which was just affordable. Until Paul's insurance money came, we were practically skint.

The villa was freezing. It had cold stone floors, bars on the windows and little furniture. Paul taught me to play bridge, and we made a four with an elderly German couple. They couldn't speak English very well, so that gave us plenty of opportunity to cheat. We played with them for hours and always came away with a few bob, which fed us the next day.

Paul never let Kim or me go with him when he went into Alicante.

'Can you bring back some English papers with you?' I begged, hoping that perhaps the case had been quashed or settled.

'Sure.' He always said, but he never brought any back.

'Didn't you get the papers?'

'There weren't any. It's a nightmare trying to get English papers round here. There's no call for them.'

Twice a day he would go up to the café to make a telephone call.

'It's impossible getting through to England in this God-forsaken country.'

'Who are you trying to ring?' We asked.

'My insurance company. They've made arrangements for me to collect some money, but it hasn't come through yet and I'm getting fed up living hand to mouth.'

'So are we.'

'More bridge!'

After a particularly good bridge evening, we decided to visit a local night club, two miles from the villa. There we met two Spanish bullfighters.

'Aren't you coming to Madrid?' They asked, offering to take Kim and me in their car to watch the big fight.

It was a good chance for Paul to get his car serviced, so the three of us decided to go with them, driving through the night. It was marvellous to reach some kind of civilisation again, to have a bath and wash ourselves at the bullfighters' hotel. We had no time to sleep that evening, as we had been invited along by the Spanish to a party given by an American.

The room was full of English and Americans, but we were so exhausted that we left to find a cheap hotel and some sleep. The next morning we decided to head back to our village. On our way to the bus stop we dropped round to say goodbye to an American we had met.

'Your name isn't Christine Keeler, is it?' he asked suddenly.

'Yes. That's right.'

'I've been reading all about you and Parliament in the *Stars and Stripes*. You're "the Missing Model"!'

'What? Me and Parliament? Don't be silly!'

'Yes. You and Parliament.'

'I don't believe you.' It sounded so strange, hearing that my name had been in the papers.

'I've got the paper upstairs. Come and see for yourself.'

We rushed upstairs and sure enough, there was an article all about how I knew Stephen and 'distinguished' people. It said that the Government were worried there might be another espionage scandal and that questions had been asked in the House. Mr John Profumo, the story went, had denied association and 'impropriety' with Miss Keeler, whose friends included Russian diplomats.

'What's impropriety?' I wondered.

'Going to bed with someone.'

'Oh, heavens! What will they do to me? I'm missing the trial. Does it say what happened? Can they put you in prison for being missing?'

'I had better go and 'phone the Consul,' Paul decided. 'I'll find out whether they can arrest you or not. Maybe they'll lock us all up.'

'Oh, what shall we do?' wailed Kim.

'Why don't you ring from here?' I asked.

'The line might be tapped.'

'Oh, surely not,' the American interrupted.

'It depends. They can get onto you fairly fast once things hot up. I'll do it outside, it'll be safer. Wait for me here.'

We stayed and talked about what the outcome might be. Paul was ages. Eventually the American said he would have to go or he'd miss a particularly good bullfight.

'But you're welcome to wait here.'

So we did.

Half-an-hour later the American returned with three pressmen and a black man. I didn't like the look of any of them.

'No, I'm not Christine Keeler,' I insisted.

'She's not,' added Kim.

But they didn't believe us, and insisted on having their story.

'Why don't you go outside with this man,' they said, indicating the black one, 'And have a cup of coffee across the road.'

'No.' I suspected they had a photographer downstairs and were going to try and get a picture of me with a coloured man.

Thankfully, Paul rang. I told him what was happening.

'Don't say anything at all. Get out as fast as you can and meet me at the Palace Hotel.'

'OK, OK,' I promised, wondering how the hell we were going to get away from this lot. They were firing their questions left and right. I pretended to compromise.

'All right. I am Christine Keeler. But I'm not going to say anything at all until that photographer you've got waiting outside has gone.'

They agreed to write a message and ordered him to 'Go back to the office. We'll call when we're ready.'

I insisted on delivering it myself, posting the card under the door to the photographer. I took the American aside and suggested that he took Kim out for a coffee, somewhere I could meet them later. He gave me the address of a bar and left with Kim. I then turned to the pressmen and said:

'All right, how about this cup of coffee?' and walked towards the door.

I walked right through that door.

'I'll be back in five minutes', I said, turning to see the three press men rise up, mouths agape.

I closed the door and rushed for the lift. Out on the street, I hailed a taxi and told him to hurry to the Palace Hotel. When I arrived Paul wasn't there, so I had to borrow money from the barman to pay the taxi.

Whilst waiting for Paul to arrive, I bought a packet of cigarettes and had a few drinks, explaining that he was due any minute. He didn't appear. An American at the bar gave me the eye. I returned his look, hoping that if the worst came to the worst, he would pay the bill and maybe help me to find Kim. He drove me round Madrid, but there was no sign of any bar bearing the name I had been given. My American was getting anxious to book me into a hotel room for his troubles, so I decided there was only one thing left I could try. It was late, and I was frightened.

'Can you give me a few pesetas? I have to go to the police station.'

He grudgingly agreed. None of the policemen understood English, so I didn't get very far. They tried looking up Hotel Keeler in the telephone directory.

163

'No. I'm the Missing Model.'

That didn't help, so they sent for an interpreter. At last they found someone at the other end of the telephone.

'Please tell them that I am Christine Keeler, the missing model. I need to speak to the British Consul.'

Having finally understood, the Spanish police stared in amazement. Within minutes another twenty had piled into the room. Unfortunately the Consul's 'phone was out of order. It was very late now, and I had no choice but to sleep in a cell or across two chairs the policemen placed together for me. I chose the latter; I was in no hurry to see the inside of a cell.

Throughout the night, the policemen kept peeping at me to make sure I was all right. In the morning the night shift took me to breakfast. Then the day shift appeared and insisted that I had breakfast with them too. A representative from the Consulate arrived after breakfast, worried and harrassed.

'Why have you kept her here?'

'I came. They didn't keep me by force. There was nowhere else for me to go. I've lost my friends and I really must get back to England. My mother will be dreadfully worried, she doesn't know where I am. My name has been in the papers, but I haven't been at the trial. I must get back and find out what has happened.'

He took me to the Consulate where Paul soon turned up.

'We can send you back by train,' they told me, 'but it looks as though you'd be better off dealing with the newspapers from here.'

Paul agreed. He took me to a flat where there were ten representatives of the *Daily Express*. They looked and acted tough. This was my first taste of what it is like to lose control of your life. My life was becoming the property of other people, and I was nothing more than a commodity to be bought or sold.

Paul and the *Express* discussed the fee all through that night and, by morning, they had a contract ready for me to sign. They would pay two thousand pounds. We both signed. Whilst Paul was talking with the reporters, one of the photograhers warned me that the contract wasn't exactly clear-cut.

'You realise, don't you, that if you and Mr Mann can't come to an agreement as to how much money he receives, the contract states that he gets fifty per cent?'

'What?' It seemed unfair. Maybe I would be arrested back in England, and Paul would then run off with *all* the money.

'I'll have to see about that.'

I didn't really believe him, but there wasn't much time to think about it. By now word had reached the other newspapers, and reporters were climbing on the roofs opposite, knocking at the door of the flat, and telephoning the whole time. One lot even hovered round in a helicopter. I was guarded by the *Express*, but nonetheless other reporters were prepared to fight to get at me. I had no idea what the fuss was really about. Of course I hadn't read Stephen's article in the *Sunday Pictorial*, nor did I know that Profumo's role in the story was running through political circles like wildfire. The reporters were shooting so many questions at me, so quickly, that no one got a proper answer.

That night thirteen of us slept in the tiny two-roomed flat, with plans the following morning to drive to the airport and escape the country.

In the car I suggested to Paul that he take twenty-five per cent of the *Express* money, knowing that he hadn't discovered that I was aware of his clause in the contract.

165

'We'll discuss it another time,' he hedged.

'No. We'll discuss it now,' I was very upset. Paul – someone I considered a friend, who I had helped out by offering somewhere to stay when he had none – was being more than devious.

We arrived at a desolate hotel, where I had been promised I could ring my Mother. Though I had sent her a postcard whilst still 'on holiday', I hadn't been in touch since.

'I must ring her at once.' But there wasn't a telephone in the hotel.

'It's a new hotel, just being built. They haven't installed one yet,' the management explained.

I was beginning to be depressed by the constant bevy of reporters. I couldn't even go to the loo without an escort. I decided to be awkward and rushed into a bedroom, locking the door behind me, so I could at least cry on my own.

'Christine, let us in.'

'No. I won't until you change the contract.'

'How?'

'Just get a new contract.'

'But we must get your photograph now, or we'll miss the deadline.'

'I'm not coming out until there's another contract.' I was determined not to cooperate until Paul was off my back, and proper arrangements were made for me to ring home.

Eventually they agreed, so I arranged with one reporter and Paul that he would receive five hundred for his trouble and I would get the balance. I thought this was fair, since Kim and I had paid nothing towards our time in Spain. Finally a new contract was drawn up and I let them photograph me.

166

'What is going to happen to me when we get back? They can't lock me up for not appearing, can they? I really didn't know it would go ahead so soon after the postponement.'

'Don't worry about anything. We'll see that you're all right. We'll fix everything up when we get back.'

Once the photographs and the story were complete, we set off again. One reporter went off with Paul and Kim and the others explained that we were going to ditch Paul. Kim was going to pick up our clothes and meet us at our next hotel.

We drove about a hundred miles to this hotel, but Paul had already got wind of their plan and had already arrived and had found my passport. There was another discussion about that, but finally the reporters got my passport back and we were ready to go. I wired my mother, and arranged for her and my step-father to meet me at a hotel in London, booked by the *Express*.

The journey to the airport was crazy. There were nine of us in the car rushing ahead, with Paul chasing us in another and rival reporters close behind. One of our tyres blew, and while some reporters covered me with a blanket so the rivals couldn't get a picture, they changed that tyre faster than a pit stop.

In moments we were charging along at a hundred miles an hour. At the airport in France, we were molested and questioned by officials. Crowds peered at me and I started to think the whole world was going mad. I was just twenty-one years old.

167

17

SECURITY

At London Airport I realised that the world *had* gone crazy. There were crowds and crowds of people waiting for a glimpse of me. Little men with cameras, babies in prams, photographers and reporters. I felt like a Martian. The *Express* reporters forged a way through the crowds, pulling me with them, and found us a cab.

It was, at least, comforting to be back in England and have a decent cup of tea. When my parents arrived at the hotel, my mother showed me a copy of Stephen's article. At last all the fuss made some sense. There was a half-page picture of me, mostly my legs, straddled by two leading stories: 'The Model, MI5, The Russian Diplomat and Me' by Stephen Ward; and, 'US Fighters Chase Red Spy Plane in Alaska Day Raid'. There I was, some kind of female James Bond. Stephen's article sickened me. He had done well for himself with choice phrases like, 'my name was dragged into the case', and 'I now find myself in a most delicate position.'

My mother had even stranger news. Apparently Michael Eddowes had been to see her.

'You'll never believe what he said.'

'Go on, for Chrissake, tell me,' I said, half expecting her to say he'd made a pass at her or something stupid.

'You won't believe me, Christine, but we had to go to the Security Police.'

'Why?' I was horrified.

'He turned up just after Mandy had left . . .'

'Mandy?'

'Yes. She came with two reporters. Of course I let her in because she's a friend of yours, but I didn't realise what it was about. "Come on, Julie," she said, "tell us where Christine is." I had your postcard, of course, but I didn't know why she wanted to know. Apparently the reporters were going to give her seventy-five pounds, "just for telling them where she is",'

'God! What's wrong with everyone? Even Paul tried to con me.' I told her all about that. 'But, anyway, tell me what Mr Eddowes came for.'

'Honestly, Christine, you won't believe me.'

'Well, tell me anyway.'

'First he asked where you were. I didn't tell him. I knew he was a friend of yours, Christine, but he didn't seem friendly towards me. You know how I am when I know someone's not being nice, I felt it straight away. So, when I wouldn't tell him, he started questioning me.'

'About what?' I interrupted.

'About everything! He started asking whether I wanted to bring the government down, just because I wouldn't listen to him.'

'What was he saying?' She took no notice.

'It all sounded so frightening. He said that someone could easily shoot from as far away as the field.'

'But why, Mum? What did he want?'

'He started by telling us how he knew all about what you'd been up to with the Russians, selling secrets. He said you'd be sent to prison for treason, or at any rate for being a spy. He said we'd read all about it in the papers. I didn't know what to believe, Christine, although I knew you weren't a spy. He said that you had proved yourself

169

guilty by running away. He kept on about it, Christine, and when he knew that I wasn't going to tell him, he started saying that the security people might come after me as well as you! Can you imagine?'

I couldn't. It was all too dreadful.

'So, after he'd gone, we called the police and they sent a security man and he told us not to worry. That it was only a try-on. But we were very worried. We've been worried to death about what's going to happen to you.'

'Well, don't worry, Mum. I'm back now.'

'And that's not all. A girl called Nina came down to ask for your address and she had reporters with her too. It's been terible, Christine, you've no idea.'

From the other papers my mother had brought, I discovered that the mini-cab driver had in fact died of a heart attack, so the trial had gone ahead on the fourteenth of March, without two major witnesses. Johnnie had been charged for slashing Lucky with intent to do grievous bodily harm. He was acquitted on that count because of lack of evidence. Secondly, he had been accused of shooting at me with intent to kill. He was acquitted again, through lack of evidence. But they sentenced him to seven years for possession of a firearm with intent to endanger life. After the verdict had been given, the court heard how he had previously been convicted for stealing, living on immoral earnings and possession of drugs. I wasn't in the least surprised.

The following day the *Daily Express* ran two front-page stories, slyly connecting me with John Profumo. 'VANISHED – Old Bailey Witness' was the headline on one side of the page. On the other was, 'WAR MINISTER SHOCK – Profumo, He Asks To Resign For Personal Reasons And Macmillan Asks Him To Stay On'. This suggested that Jack had offered his resignation, which he hadn't. Underneath was a statement from him denying the report.

That might have been the end of it, but for two men. John Lewis and, through him, the Labour MP George Wigg had my evidence about the affair on tape. Neither of *them* were going to let the matter drop. Lewis, I know now, had a bitter personal grudge against Stephen. Wigg's quarrel was with Profumo, who had humiliated him in Parliament over Army policy. And they both wanted public confidence in the Conservative Government's ability to maintain the security of the country shaken. With any luck, the loss of seats would let Labour in. We were starting to hear about 'thirteen years of Tory misrule'.

John Lewis had hoped that matters would come to a head at Johnnie Edgecombe's trial; that, at the very least, the trial would be postponed until I had been found. He put about a rumour that I had been smuggled out of the country by Profumo. The press, however, who got their fingers burned for failing to reveal their sources in the recent Vassall spy enquiry, were cautious about spreading too many unsubstantiated stories.

In Parliament, Wigg suggested the trial had been dealt with abnormally and requested an inquiry to find out how many trials had proceeded without a key witness for the Crown being present. Again my name was linked with John Profumo, this time on the *Daily Mail*'s front page: 'Commons Questions Stopped on Missing Model' was accompanied by a piece speculating on the future of the War Minister.

On the 21st March, George Wigg stood up during a debate on the Vassall enquiry and suggested that there might be another similar case brewing.

'There is not an Honourable Member in the House, nor a journalist in the Press Gallery, nor do I believe is there a person in the public gallery who, in the past few days, has not heard rumour upon rumour involving a member of Government Front Bench.'

Using his parliamentary privilege he asked the Home Secretary to go to the Despatch Box and deny the rumours about 'Miss Christine Keeler, Miss Davies and a shooting by a West Indian.' And Barbara Castle added that if anyone did know where Christine Keeler was, it was their duty to own up.

'If accusations are made that there are people in high places who do know and are not informing the police, is it not a matter of public interest?'

The Chief Whip called Jack Profumo to his rooms early in the morning, and they worked out a statement for him to read.

Soon after eleven o'clock the next day, John Profumo addressed the House.

'I understand that my name has been connected with the rumours about the disappearance of Miss Keeler. I would like to take this opportunity of making a personal statement about these matters. I last saw Miss Keeler in December, 1961 and I have not seen her since. I have no idea where she is now.

'Any suggestion that I was in any way connected with or responsible for her absence from the trial at the Old Bailey is wholly and completely untrue.

'My wife and I first met Miss Keeler at a house party in July, 1961 at Cliveden. Among a number of people there was Dr Stephen Ward, whom we already knew slightly, and a Mr Ivanov, who was an attaché at the Russian Embassy.

'The only other occasion that my wife or I met Mr Ivanov was for a moment at the official reception for Major Gagarin at the Soviet Embassy.

'My wife and I had a standing invitation to visit Dr

Ward. Between July and December, 1961, I met Miss Keeler on about half a dozen occasions at Dr Ward's flat, when I called to see him and his friends. Miss Keeler and I were on friendly terms. There was no impropriety whatsoever in my acquaintanceship with Miss Keeler.

'Mr Speaker, I have made this personal statement because of what was said in the House last evening by the three Hon. Members, and which, of course, was protected by privilege. I shall not hesitate to issue writs for libel and slander if scandalous allegations are made or repeated outside the House.'

Still they weren't satisfied. George Wigg announced on Panorama that it was still a matter of national security. Stephen contacted Wigg after the programme, and went to see him the following day to explain what really had happened; how he had been in touch with the Security Service himself, and only too willing to help settle matters between the East and the West. The scandal was losing Stephen business, and he was desperate to clear it up as quickly as possible. George Wigg noted it all down in a memorandum.

It wasn't long after I had got back from Spain, that I made my first appearance at the Old Bailey. I arrived, accompanied by *Daily Express* reporter, to be greeted by crowds of people longing for a look, as though I was some kind of freak. I was terrified. The moment I got out the taxi, the police came forward and carved a passage for me through that surging, sweating crowd. I looked up the stairs of the Old Bailey and to my horror found the face of Lucky Gordon waiting for me.

'No! No! I'm not going up there!'

Lucky came towards me.

'I love the girl! I love the girl!' cried Lucky, as five policemen rushed forward to hold him off.

173

'Stop him! Please, stop him! He'll murder me!' I cried, unable to escape because of the crowds all round me.

The police dragged him off.

'I love her! I love her!' I heard him cry, until the heavy doors of the Old Bailey closed behind me.

It was so vast inside that building, my legs shook. I had no idea that I would soon become used to being there. For now, all I received was a straight forty-pound fine for not being present at Johnny's trial.

I didn't know where to turn. Everyone seemed to have deserted me, and I felt I was too hot to expect anyone to want to have me around. Though matters had quietened down, I don't think anyone believed they were over. In desperation I went to stay with Paula Hamilton-Marshall.

I bumped into an old friend of Stephen's, Robin Drury, who rang me one day and asked if I could lend him ninety pounds to pay a drugs charge.

'As we're both in the same boat,' he said, 'I thought you might help me out.'

Of course I lent him the money, though later I wished I hadn't.

It wasn't long before the police turned up on the doorstep looking for me. I wondered what I had done this time.

'It's a matter of security, Christine. We have to ask you a few questions,' explained my old friend Detective-Sergeant Burrows. With him was his superior, Chief Inspector Samuel Herbert.

'What's a matter of security?'

'This business about you knowing Eugene Ivanov and John Profumo. We need the facts. You want to help your country, don't you?'

'Yes, of course.'

'You must realise the position you are in. You could

174

have been spying. That's how it might appear. It's possible you could get three years in prison, but if you want to help your country, clearly there would be no reason.'

'Of course I'll come,' I agreed, confident that these two men were on my side, obviously trying to protect me now, though they had done nothing, despite endless pleading 'phone calls from me before the trial, to protect me from Lucky Gordon.

The main thing that interested them was that Stephen had asked me to get information from John Profumo.

'How was it exactly? Do you remember the date?'

Of course I didn't, it had all happened two years ago.

'Where were you at the time? Did you see Profumo or Ivanov afterwards?'

The whole thing seemed ridiculous. As soon as the police left, I rang Stephen. Although there was a major rift between us, I thought he ought to know about this latest development.

'Stephen, they think I was spying!' I was frantic.

'Oh, don't be so silly, little baby.' He brushed it aside. 'What are you doing tonight?' He asked.

'Nothing.'

'Well, come round. I want to introduce you to a good friend of mine, a film producer.'

When I arrived there were three other people there.

'Look, little baby,' Stephen excitedly told me, 'They're going to make a film about what's happened. I'm going to sign. Will you?'

Stephen seemed very distant. Even his 'little baby' didn't ring true. I looked dubious.

'Look, they'll give you three thousand pounds, and five per cent of the gross profits! Isn't that marvellous?'

I wasn't sure about this.

'Don't be silly, Christine,' he insisted.

175

I signed and stayed to watch Stephen help put together a rough outline for the script, naturally putting most of the blame on me.

The following day he rang again.

'Why don't we do a book together?'

More plans. It was typical of Stephen, except now I wanted nothing to do with it.

Then Burrows and Herbert were round again with more questions. They had with them a plan of the inside of John Profumo's house.

'It would have been quite easy for you,' they pointed out, 'to have gone into Mr Profumo's office and taken away papers whilst he was in the bathroom.'

'But I didn't.'

'Well somehow we've got to prove what you were doing there.'

'You *know*. I've already told you. I saw him quite a few times. I liked him. There was nothing else to it. Nothing to do with spies or any connection with Eugene.'

'And can you remember Eugene and John Profumo meeting at all?'

'Yes. At Cliveden.'

'But not on any other occasion? They must have met quite often at Stephen's flat? Have you been there recently?'

'I saw Stephen last night.'

'Why?'

'He wanted to see me about a film script. They're going to make a film about what's happened and they're giving me three thousand pounds and five per cent of the gross profits.'

'I don't advise you to continue your relationship with Stephen,' warned short, thick-set Herbert.

Burrows interrupted:

'To return to your relationship with Mr Profumo, we must be quite certain that you had no opportunity to go into his office. Now, tell me quite truthfully, did you on any occasion go into his office? We'll quite understand if you say yes. It won't necessarily mean you're in any trouble. These people have ways and means of forcing a person to do things against their will, and all this will be taken into consideration.'

'No. I didn't go in. Why should I?'

'But, looking at this plan of the house, it would have been quite easy for you to have gone into his office whilst he was in the bathroom.'

'But I didn't.'

'There must have been some reason for you to have gone to his house in the first place?'

'He took me there.'

'But why to his house? Did you specifically ask to go there?'

'No. I didn't.'

'Then why to his house? Why not to Stephen's?'

'He said he didn't want to be at Stephen's. He wanted to show me his house. He told me it was one of the Nash buildings. That's a famous architect.'

'So no one suggested you visited his house?'

'No, he suggested it.'

'Stephen?'

'No, Jack just took me there.'

'And Eugene Ivanov didn't suggest that you get access to his house? That somehow you would arrange things so that you visited Mr Profumo's house?'

'No.'

'Think very carefully. You see they might not have wanted you to do anything except describe the house, where the rooms were.'

'But no one knew. I hardly saw Eugene at all after that

177

weekend. He stayed away because he was embarrassed. He had been going on all that evening about how upright and straight Russians were, and then . . . well, he fell into it – so he didn't dare look me in the face afterwards.'

'And you didn't tell anyone about going to the house?'

'I told Stephen, of course.'

'You told Stephen?' Herbert pricked his ears up.

'Of course I told Stephen. Don't you understand? Stephen was my friend? I told him practically everything.'

'And did you describe the house in detail to him?'

'I can't remember. It was too long ago.'

'Try and remember. Did you describe the interior of the house in detail?'

'No, I can't remember.'

'And do you remember whether it was before your visit to this house, or afterwards, that Stephen suggested that you ask John Profumo when the Americans were going to give the bomb to West Germany?'

'I can't remember. I think it was afterwards. It might have been before.'

'Did he suggest that you find out by having a look at Mr Profumo's papers yourself, without asking him?'

'No. He didn't. He didn't ask like that at all. It was a joke. It didn't mean anything.'

'Did Eugene Ivanov ever ask you about this bomb?'

'Of course not.'

'But when Stephen asked, what did you say?'

'I can't remember.'

'Try and remember. When Stephen asked you to find out from Mr Profumo when West Germany would receive nuclear arms, can't you remember what you replied?'

'It wasn't like that. It was just a joke. I said, "Don't be silly, Stephen, I could never do anything like that." And that was it.'

'When did he ask you?'

'I can't remember.'

'Well, you must be able to remember the circumstances. Were you at a party?'

'No.'

'Where were you?'

'I don't remember.'

Burrows changed the subject to other occasions when I had been with John Profumo.

'Did he take you inside the War Ministry when he showed you where it was?'

'Of course not.'

'Did he go in and fetch any papers, or for any other reason?'

'No. He just drove me around London and showed me where he worked.'

'He didn't go in?'

'No.'

'You didn't wait in the car for him to go in and fetch something? Try and remember.'

'No, we just drove past.'

'And on any other occasion?'

'There wasn't another occasion. He only drove past with me once.'

'Why?'

'Because he was showing me where he worked.'

'Why do you think he was going to show you where he worked.'

'Because he thought I might be interested.'

'And you were?'

'Yes, of course I was.'

'Who had suggested you were taken to see the War Ministry? That Mr Profumo take you there, maybe show you around?'

179

'No one.'

'It wasn't suggested by Eugene Ivanov that you visit the War Ministry. Maybe even get a job there as a secretary or anything like that?'

'No!' I could guess the next question.

'And Stephen didn't suggest that you work at the War Ministry?'

'No.'

Again the subject was changed by Herbert, who I now considered a thoroughly nasty type. We were back to Stephen and the bomb. Herbert had a mean look. He questioned me rapidly, giving me no time to think nor enough time to finish what I was saying. Burrows was the kind, gentle one. They took it in turn to ask questions. When I got angry and cross with Herbert, Burrows took over. When I got bored and sleepy with answering Burrows, Herbert had another go.

I was usually interrogated in the same bare room, with a table and hideously uncomfortable school chairs. When they came to fetch me at the flat, I naturally accompanied them. I still trusted the good old British copper.

'You must remember when Stephen asked you,' Herbert glared.

'I think it was after.'

'The weekend at Cliveden?'

'Yes.'

'After your affair with Eugene Ivanov?'

'I didn't have an . . .'

'After visiting Mr Profumo's house?'

'I can't remember. I think so.'

'Where did he ask you?'

'I can't remember.'

'Where you outside?'

'It might have been in the garden.'

'Garden?'

'At the cottage, Stephen loved gardening . . .'

'At the weekend? After Cliveden, or at the same time?'

'Yes. At the weekend.'

'Not during the week?'

'No, Stephen worked during the week.'

'He asked you in the garden?'

'He might have done. Or we might have been in bed. I think we were in . . .'

'But you have denied a sexual relationship with Stephen.'

'Yes.'

'But you just said, "We might have been in bed."'

'Well, we might have been.'

'So, you are contradicting yourself. Let's have the truth.'

'I didn't have anything to do with him in that way.'

Herbert grinned.

'You must have had something to do with him.'

'No, I never had. We were just like brother and sister.'

'Oh! Ha, Ha! Come on, Christine. You can't kid me. I'm a big boy now.'

'I didn't.'

'Just once?'

'No, not just once. I didn't at all.'

'In the beginning?'

'He tried in the very beginning, but I never did.'

'So it was in bed that he asked you about the bomb?'

'I think so.'

'And what did he say?'

'Just, "Wouldn't it be funny?"'

'Funny?'

'Yes. It was a joke. He said now that we know both the Russian and the War Minister, it would be a laugh.'

'And you replied?'

181

'I didn't think it so funny, really.'

'What did you say to Stephen Ward?'

'Nothing. I can't remember. Just "No."'

'No? No, to what?'

'No, it wasn't very funny and I wouldn't.'

'Wouldn't what?'

'Wouldn't ask John Profumo when the West Germans were getting the bomb.'

'And?'

'And nothing. That's all there is to it.'

Eventually they let me go. Four o'clock in the morning, dead tired and bored with the whole game.

18

FRAME

THE BLANK walls were depressing. The hard chair made me ache and the bright lights soon made me tired. I looked at their familiar faces. This was the twelfth time they had interviewed me this week. I knew those faces better than my own. Burrows sat in his pinstripes, absorbing the questions and answers in silence. I felt that Burrows was on my side, probably the only person in the world who was, but I hated Herbert with his full face, fair hair and darting eyes. He was always dressed in tweeds. I didn't dare displease either of them by refusing to answer their questions because I knew that the police stuck together.

'Why haven't you bought any new clothes, Christine?' Herbert looked at my dress. Last year's style.

'I don't often buy new clothes.'

'But now you've got that money from the newspaper, surely you've bought some new clothes?'

'No. I've paid bills. I haven't bought anything much. Cigarettes. Eye-lashes. Why?'

'Where have you put the money?'

'In the bank.'

'And other money you've received?'

'What other money?'

'Large sums you've received before. We know all about it. But you're clever enough not to buy new things, not to flaunt your money. Where does it go to?'

'I don't understand.'

'Who gets a share in it?'

'What do you mean?'

'You must have been given considerable portions of cash before. The press has not been your only source of income. I am asking you what you have done with the money. There is no point in you trying to hide the fact, because we can have a thorough search made until it's found.'

'But I haven't got any money, except what the *Express* paid me.'

'Now don't tell me that one, Christine. Or have they been keeping the money for you in another country?'

'They?'

'The people, Christine, who have been paying you for getting information.' Herbert was getting angry.

'There aren't any people.'

'Now we know that isn't true. We know how clever you are to hide it. Most girls suddenly coming into some money, as you claim, would have gone out and spent a good deal of it in dress shops.'

'Well, I'm not like that. And I don't understand what you're getting at. I've told you, I had nothing to do with being a spy.'

The interrogation ended there, but they were back again a few days later.

'We have some questions to ask you, Christine. Can you come with us?'

'Wait a moment. I've got to do my hair.'

They waited until I was ready, then escorted me downstairs into the waiting car and I was driven to my little room with its painted brick walls.

'When did you meet Bill Astor?' Herbert asked a new question.

'I hardly knew him.' I was astonished at the turn the questioning had taken.

'But you've met him at Cliveden?'

'Oh yes. But I didn't know him really well. Hardly at all.'

'You must have had sex with him?'

'What?' I could hardly believe I was hearing this.

'Well?'

'No! I did not.' What were they getting at?

'You must have done,' Herbert insisted.

'I did not.'

'Come on, Christine. Who did you go to bed with then if not Stephen, nor Bill Astor?'

I was speechless.

'Come on now, Christine. You must have had something to do with Bill Astor?'

'No, I didn't.'

'You had a flat with Mandy Rice-Davies?'

'Yes.' I was amazed they knew so much about me. 'But why are you asking me all these questions? I don't under-stand.'

I had tried as far as possible to answer truthfully everything they had asked me about the bomb so that neither Stephen nor I, nor Jack for that matter, would get into trouble over a security issue that didn't exist except in the minds of a few people who needed an issue to make trouble for the Conservatives. But why this constant probing into my private life? I didn't see how that had anything to do with security.

'Well you see, Christine, we've been after Stephen Ward for eleven years now, and we, that is Mr Burrows and myself, have been put in charge of finding out what all this business is about.'

'You've been after him for eleven years?'

'Yes.'

'Why? What for?'

'How do you think he got his practice?'

'I don't know. How?'

'Christine,' Burrows intervened, 'I personally have watched Stephen Ward for years. He has always used young girls to get him things, and a number of other matters he's involved with which I can't tell you about.' He sounded very convincing.

'Christine, that man is no good. He's a bad lot,' Herbert shouted.

My head was reeling. Perhaps Stephen was a spy, not an Englishman at all. It seemed to make sense. Then I remembered about Vickie Martin, a girl Stephen had often talked about. She was killed in a car accident. Maybe he had wanted to get rid of her.

'So you see,' Herbert continued ruthlessly, 'You must tell us everything. Maybe you were lucky. But Stephen Ward has used young girls for many years. Used them,' he was shouting.

Why should I not believe them? They had been keeping an eye on Stephen for eleven years, yet it seemed quite fantastic that I had become involved in a web of espionage.

Satisfied that he had got through to me, Herbert continued:

'We need to know the names and circumstances of every man you have ever had anything to do with. Just in case . . .'

'Just in case,' Burrows continued, 'any one of them had a Russian background. You can never tell until a thorough investigation has been carried out. They're very clever.'

'Let's begin with going to Spain. Paul Mann suggested it, didn't he?'

'I don't know. Both Paul and Kim were going.'

'What about money?'

'Paul had some from an insurance company. He was going to collect it in Spain, so we didn't have much.'

'You had some? Where did it come from?'

'I didn't have much. A little left from the *Sunday Pictorial* and I borrowed twenty pounds from a friend.'

'A friend? A man friend?'

'Yes.'

'Who was he?'

'I don't remember.'

'You must remember. You slept with him for it?'

'No, I did not.' I was furious. Those dirty-minded police.

'So he just lent you twenty pounds?'

'Yes.'

'You must remember his name.'

'I don't,' I said, though I knew perfectly well. It was in fact a friend of Stephen's who ran a bridge club. But I didn't see why I should sign another statement saying, 'So and So lent me twenty pounds to go to Spain, and I didn't have sex with him.' It was so utterly stupid. What business was it of theirs who I slept with?

'Paul Mann suggested going to Spain?'

'Yes, but it was my decision to go. Everything had become too much, you know,' I looked at Burrows. 'I kept telephoning you because someone had rung and threatened that two black men were waiting for an opportunity to beat me up. And there was all that trouble with Lucky. I would have been killed. It was a good job I did go.'

'You must remember how much money he lent you.'

'Yes, twenty pounds.'

'Are you sure it wasn't more? Are you sure you can't remember who it was?'

'Yes, I am sure.'

'Perhaps it was Mr Profumo.'

'No, it wasn't.'

'Stephen Ward?'

'No.'

'Lord Astor?'

'No. The chap didn't even know I was going abroad. He had nothing to do with any of this.'

They gave up and took me home, realising that I was fed up and sick of them, too tired to be of any further help that night.

They came again the next day to take me to MI5. First they drove me round and round London.

'You're going to see Commander Townsend. You may tell him everything you know. Answer all his questions. This is a matter of security.'

We arrived at a large building and went up to the top floor in a lift. We were kept waiting in an outer office for a few moments only. Burrows and Herbert were as nervous as I was. We walked in to confront three new faces. Commander Townsend was sitting, the other two stood on either side of him. He asked me the usual questions.

'Did you ever have anything to do with Eugene Ivanov?'

'Yes, once.'

'And Profumo?'

'Yes.'

'How often?'

'Not very often.'

'Were you ever in his office alone?'

'No.'

'How many times did you go to his house?'

'Twice, I think.'

'Did Stephen Ward ask you to find out from John Profumo if nuclear warheads were going to be given to West Germany?'

'No.'

This came as a surprise. Commander Townsend raised an eyebrow.

'He just said that the Americans were going to give Germany the bomb, and wouldn't it be a good thing if I was to find out when?'

'Did you try?'

'No, of course not. I said to Stephen something like, "Don't be silly, as if Jack would ever tell me anything." Then he laughed and said he was only joking, but now I don't think he was.'

'Didn't you report this to anyone at the time?'

'Well, yes. One day at the cottage – Eugene was there, I think, there were quite a few people – and Eugene was talking amongst them all. Stephen was weeding and I said to him, "I think Eugene's a spy." "Well, there's a lot of money to be made in it, little baby," he said. I put it out of my head after that.'

'Do you think Stephen is a spy?'

'Yes, sort of. He is a Communist sympathiser and he also likes to impress. I think that if he had been able to find out anything, he would have done.'

Commander Townsend then asked Burrows and Herbert to leave the room.

'I have some more questions to ask you, but it is very important that you never tell anyone what I have to say next. Not even the police. Nobody. Do you understand?'

'Yes.'

'You have met Mr John Lewis?'

'Yes. I was introduced to him at a party Paul and I went to. Mr Lewis said he would get me a solicitor for the Johnnie Edgecombe trial so that he could intervene if questions were asked about friends of mine in the past. He kept asking me about Profumo and Ivanov.'

'Did he get you a solicitor?'

189

'Yes.'

'Can you tell me who?'

'Yes. In fact his office is just across the square,' I pointed.

'How do you know where you are?' His two aides looked shocked.

'I have a very good sense of direction.'

'And who else knows about this?'

'Michael Eddowes.'

'Anything other than you've told me?'

'Nothing else. But neither Mr Lewis nor Mr Eddowes know what I've just told you, that Stephen said there was money in it.'

I was politely shown out and Herbert and Burrows took me back to the station for more questions.

The next time they came for me, I decided to take my own car.

'So that I can leave,' I told Herbert.

'I'm fed up with telling the local constables you've got a driving licence, Christine. So please will you get one?' Herbert insisted as I drove him to the police station.

'We need some details about your other boyfriends, Christine,' Burrows explained kindly, whilst Herbert was out of the room, fetching me a cup of tea.

'Well, I had a Greek boyfriend for a long time, while I was working at Murrays, and before. He was after my boyfriend back home.'

'His name?'

I gave them his name.

'But I haven't seen him for years and years. It was all such a long time ago.'

'And while you were at the Club?'

'Well, there was Stephen, but that was different. Stephen was always there. I didn't really have a boyfriend when I was with him, until I went to live with Sherry.'

'Sherry?'

'A girlfriend. Stephen was looking for a larger place for he and I to live in, and we went to see Peter . . .'

'Peter?' Herbert had returned.

'That must be Peter Rachman. You lived with him?'

'He was in the house business and Stephen thought he could get us a house cheaply. But I met Sherry, who lived in one of Peter's houses and she asked me to come and live with her.'

'How long were you there?'

'Some months, I can't remember. But I had to leave when Peter got possessive. He wouldn't even let me see my mother for the weekend. He came and took the car away.'

'Car?'

'He'd given me this car . . .'

'Why?'

'Because he liked me, I suppose.'

'Did he give you anything else? Were you paying rent?'

'Rent? At his flat?'

'Yes. With Sherry. How did you manage? Were you working?'

'No. It was Sherry's flat, or her boyfriend Raymond's – Peter let them have it. I just stayed there with Sherry. Raymond was often away and Sherry and I lived there together. We saw Peter quite a lot. He was very kind. Every time he bought me a dress, he got one for Sherry as well, because Raymond was away.'

'How old were you then?'

'Oh, eighteen, I suppose.'

'And what did you do for money?'

'Peter gave me some each week. He always carried a lot on him.'

'How much?'

'About a hundred pounds sometimes.'

191

'He gave you a hundred pounds?'

'No. No. He gave me about twenty.'

'Each week?'

'Yes. While I was there.'

'You were his mistress?'

'I don't know. I mean he didn't live with me. He was never there at night. Yes, I suppose so. He came in the afternoon.'

'And Stephen introduced you to him.'

'I met him through Stephen, yes.'

'Did Stephen ask you to go and live with Sherry?'

'Oh, no. Stephen didn't like it at all. He was very angry and telephoned Peter to say so.'

'So we can say,' Herbert was making notes, 'that you went to live with Peter Rachman for about six months, and that he gave you twenty pounds a week and a car.'

'No, that's wrong. I went to live with Sherry, but it was Peter's flat. He didn't live there. He just came and went until we had this row about me going to see my boyfriend in the country.'

'Which one was that?'

'Another Peter. I'd known him for years and liked him very much. Peter Rachman was angry because he wanted me to be with him whenever he wanted. So he took the car away and told me to get out, or to start seeing things differently. So I went back to Stephen.'

'Who did Stephen introduce you to next?'

'What do you mean?'

'Did you leave Stephen again, and go and live with someone else that he had introduced you to?'

'No. I can't remember. I lived with Mandy for a while.'

'Whereabouts?'

'In Comeragh Road. We had a flat there.'

'What job were you doing then?'

192

'We decided to chuck it in at the club – I'd met Mandy working there.'

'And Stephen introduced Mandy to Peter Rachman?'

'No.'

What did it matter who introduced who, and to whom?

'How did Mandy meet Peter?'

'We bumped into him.'

'With Stephen?'

'No. I knew him, so when we met him at a party and she was keen on him, I invited him round to the flat to meet her. And it worked out very well, they got on well together.'

'I see. Who else visited your flat?'

'Lots of people.'

'Stephen brought people there?'

'I can't remember. He may have done.'

'Who paid the rent?'

'We did.'

'What job did you have?'

'We weren't working then.'

'So where did you get the money to pay the rent?'

'I can't remember. My boyfriend gave me some at the beginning.'

'Which boyfriend was that?'

Herbert was firing questions and I didn't fancy his tone of voice.

'I don't remember. We had some modelling jobs and paid the rent like that.'

'You went to America?' Herbert glared.

'Yes.'

'Why?'

'Mandy and Nina Gadd were going, though as it turned out, Nina never got there.'

'You went for a holiday?'

'Yes.'

'Who paid for that trip?'

'I can't remember.' Why the hell should I tell them?

'You must remember. It must have been a very expensive flight. In Stephen Ward's article, he said some friend had payed for your return.'

'I can't remember. It was a boyfriend of mine.'

'What was his name?'

'I can't remember.'

'You went to America, and can't remember who paid for your ticket? Come, come, Christine, you don't expect me to believe that?'

Herbert stared at me accusingly, trying to bully me into submission. I knew Michael wasn't in any way involved, so there was no need to drag him in now. Sometimes they made me so angry, those two.

'His name was Michael.'

But I wouldn't tell them his surname.

'You needn't worry about giving us their names, Christine,' soothed Burrows.

'If none of these people are involved, it will only help to clear their names if they are innocent, and of course to help clear yours too.'

I still wouldn't tell them. It was the least I could do for Michael.

13

RESIGNATION

I WAS sure now that it was Stephen they were after. Every question related to him, every detail about him excited them. However he had betrayed me – even if he was a spy – I had to warn him now.

When I got home that night, I called him.

'Stephen, the police, I think they're after you. They keep on asking questions always about you. I'm sure they're after you.'

'Don't be silly, little baby. I haven't done anything wrong.'

'I don't know, Stephen, but they're after you.'

'Don't be ridiculous, Christine. There's nothing for anyone to be after me for. You're imagining things.'

'I'm not, Stephen.'

'Look,' he carried on. 'Why don't you come round? We should do this book together. We'd make a good deal of money out of it.'

'No, I don't want to.'

I'd had enough of him using me to try and clear his name. I didn't care whether I annoyed Stephen any more. I was adamant.

Stephen had indeed changed since the shooting. He'd become dirty, slovenly and unkempt. Even when I first met him he seldom bathed: 'It's bad for your skin to bath too often,' he said, but now I don't think he really bothered to wash at all. Before he had always been immaculately dressed, kept his hands beautifully and was always clean-shaven with that charming smile. Now, he wasn't bothering to wear a suit and the flesh on his face had fallen. He looked as though he hardly slept.

On the few occasions I rang he was always out, or just going out. I had heard that he only lived for 'scenes'. Scenes with West Indians, prostitutes, down-and-outs. Each one more depraved than the last. The only gentlemen he met now had themselves fallen on hard times. All his other friends in high places had deserted him. He had relied on their support, but they had let him down. The Establishment he had entertained for so many years, who had 'dropped in' for a cup of coffee or a chat at any time of day or night, had turned him out, turned against him. They threatened or ignored him. His friends, like mine, had proved false.

Mandy and I, as well as many other people we knew, had told Stephen that the police were continuing their enquiries into his activities. He got very upset and decided to get in touch with the Prime Minister's Principal Private Secretary, Timothy Bligh. He suggested that if the police weren't called off him, the only thing left for him to do would be to tell the truth about Jack Profumo and me.

The police continued their investigations. So Stephen wrote more letters to the Home Secretary, to his own MP and one to Harold Wilson.

To Wilson, the Leader of the Opposition, Stephen wrote:

'Obviously my efforts to conceal the fact that Mr Profumo had not told the truth in Parliament have made it look as if I myself had something to hide. It is quite clear now that they must wish the facts to be known, and I shall see that they are.'

What more could Wilson want? He of course sent the letter to the Prime Minister, Harold Macmillan, as if to say, 'I told you so' and demanded a further and fuller enquiry into the security aspects. This was done, but the answer came back that the Security Service had not been informed about 'Mr Profumo's alleged visits to Ward or to Miss Keeler.'

To quote Lord Denning's Report, 'Mr Wilson found it necessary to pursue the matter further.' Wilson, probably in the light of George Wigg's memorandum taken at his meeting with Stephen, was disturbed by the reply and requested a meeting with the Prime Minister. In Macmillan's room in the House, Harold Wilson told him that if the Government were not going to act, then he reserved the right to bring up the matter in the House. Macmillan once again assured Wilson there were no unresolved security problems, but to make absolutely sure, he would ask the security authorities to check again.

The Lord Chancellor opened the enquiry on 30th May. The following day, Parliament went into recess and John Profumo was warned that he would be interviewed the following week. He and his wife Valerie decided to spend the week in Venice. The press knew something was up. This time Jack had *his* full share of reporters and cameras as he flew out of London Airport.

Jack returned from holiday almost straight away, having decided to make a clean breast of things. He flew back to London with Valerie on Sunday, and on Tuesday saw the Chief Whip and the Prime Minister's Private Secretary and confessed. To Harold Macmillan he wrote:

'In my statement I said that there had been no impropriety in this association. To my very deep regret I have to admit that this was not true, and that I misled you, and my colleagues, and the House. I ask you to

197

understand that I did this to protect, as I thought, my wife and family, who were equally misled, as were my professional advisers.'

* * * * *

By way of thanks for having lent him ninety pounds to pay his drugs charge, Robin Drury kept in touch with me. He often came to Paula's flat and one day he suggested that he act as my manager and that we should make some money by writing a book.

I agreed. Robin had stuck with me throughout, and seemed a good friend. We put the book down on tape. Robin put methadrine in my coffee to make me talk more – and I did: it was a good way of getting the story down. Not too much hard work, just talking and answering his questions.

I saw Robin the day after Jack's resignation was announced. Robin had heard from the *News of the World*, who wanted to buy my life story for £23,000. So much was happening suddenly. Reporters were asking more questions:

'Where did you live as a child?'
'Who was your first boyfriend?'
'Where did you go to school?'
'What do your parents do?'
'Why did you come to London?'
'What was the Cabaret Club like?'

They wrote the answers in the first person, as though I had written the story.

Whilst all *that* was going on, Lucky turned up at Paula's flat. Her brother opened the door and there was some kind of scuffle. When I told Burrows and Herbert, they said they could put him away for a week, for mental observation, but nothing more unless he provoked more trouble. Anything was a relief. But no sooner had they taken Lucky in, than my good friend Stephen bailed him out. He had other plans for Lucky.

Burrows and Herbert still persisted in their enquiries. One day, Burrows opened the session.

'This is a very grave matter, Christine.'

'What? What's happened?'

'You never told us about your trips to the Russian Embassy.'

'What? Which trips?'

I'd completely forgotten that I'd ever been there.

'We've been informed that you visited the Russian Embassy and delivered something.'

It came back to me in a rush. With relief that there had been nothing more to it; I told them the story.

'Stephen asked me to deliver a letter to Eugene once. No, twice I think.'

'Twice?'

'Yes. I drove once to deliver the letter.'

'What was in it?'

'I didn't look.' Stephen said it was a note telling Eugene he couldn't make it for bridge that evening.'

'I see. Why didn't you mention this before?'

'I didn't remember.'

'A pity.' Then Herbert stared at me.

'It might have saved you and us a lot of trouble.'

'Why is it so important? It was only a message. I didn't see anyone there. I didn't even read the message.'

'It proves you were an accomplice.'

'How? I mean Stephen isn't a *real* spy. Nor am I. We're just not.'

'Did Eugene ever give you any money?'

'What for?'

'Anything.'

'No. Of course not.'

'Try and remember.'

'I've told you. I can remember perfectly well, he never gave me any money. Why should he?'

'Did he give Stephen money?'

'I don't know, why don't you ask Stephen?'

'Stephen must have mentioned it.'

'No he didn't. Why should he?'

'You were living with him, how did he pay his bills?'

'I don't know, with money, I suppose.'

'Where did he get his money from?'

'Sometimes he sold his drawings, quite often in fact.'

'No other income?'

'I don't know much about it.'

'Did Stephen always have a lot of money? Did he flash it around?'

'*What?* Never! Stephen is very mean, you know. He doesn't even offer to buy drinks or pay the restaurant bill, if anyone else will.'

'So his income came from selling his paintings?'

'Oh, come off it. He has his practice as well.'

'Did he work hard?'

'Sometimes. It depended on whether there were a lot of patients.'

'And you used to meet all the patients?'

'No.'

'You met most of them?'

'No. I really don't know.'

'You showed them in. Made appointments for them?'

'No. I didn't go to the consultancy. Occasionally a patient might ring Stephen at home, in which case I might take a message. That's all.'

'Bill Astor was a patient?'

'Yes. But not in London. Stephen used to treat Bill at the weekend in Cliveden.'

'And you went with him?'

'No, never. Stephen always went alone.'

'Lord Astor visited you in your flat in Comeragh Road? Stephen brought him along, as well as other people?'

'No, he never went there. I saw him just before I went to Spain.'

'He lent you money to go to Spain?'

'No. No. No. He said he might help me to get a barrister. He never knew about going to Spain, that was afterwards.'

On and on they went. Sometimes I was kept there for eight hours or more going over the same ground, again and again. Suddenly they would spring another revelation on me.

'It was your gun. Where did you get it from?'

'Look. You can knock my head against a brick wall, but I will never tell you.'

I wasn't going to get any more people into trouble.

On one of the rare evenings relaxing at Paula's, her brother John and I had a row – I can't remember now what it was about. Anyway I slapped his face and, hitting back at me, he cut my eye. Then he stormed out. After he had gone, Paula and I decided to go out for the evening with two West Indian friends who had dropped round.

We went downstairs, but waiting for us outside in the street we found Lucky Gordon. Stephen had told him where I was. He pounced on me, pushing me back into the building. He was punching my face and shouting abuse. Paula rushed upstairs to ring the police, while Lucky had me on the ground, kicking me in the ribs and chest, and on legs. My eye was now bleeding profusely and I could barely see. The two West Indians stood by stupefied. Then suddenly stirred into action, one pulled Lucky off me. I leapt up and ran upstairs, leaving my handbag spilled over the hall floor.

'Let me in!' I screamed.

'It's all right. The police are on their way,' said Paula, leading me into the sitting-room and locking the door of the flat behind us. Olive, the housekeeper, took me into the bathroom to wash the blood that was pouring from my eye. The sight of my own blood made me even angrier.

The West Indians had returned with my handbag. On hearing that the police were coming, they were keen to be off. I was letting Olive patch up my eye. One of the guys was on bail and waiting trial. The other was worried that if he got mixed up in any trouble he would lose his flat. He had six children and it wasn't worth the risk. The police might get nasty seeing he was coloured.

Before they left, Herbert and Burrows arrived.

'Quick! Hide in the bedroom!' said Paula.

The two policemen walked in and took our statements. They were delighted to have a reason for charging Lucky. They called for a doctor to confirm the damage done. Lucky had long since disappeared, but they found him the following morning.

After the police left, Paula and I sat up for ages.

'I don't want people locked up. I don't think that's the answer. I could have had Lucky put away three times, but I didn't. This time I must.'

'It'll mean another court case . . .'

'I know. But I shall be here for this one.'

I just hoped that once Lucky was well and truly out of the way, I might be able to pick up the scraps of my life again. At least I would be able to move without fear.

When Herbert and Burrows called next, I was in no mood for their questions.

'Yes. He had some girlfriends, but not when I was there.'

'Mandy stayed there?'

'Yes.'

'And gave him money?'

'I think so. Nina Gadd stayed too and paid him rent.'

'How much money did you give Stephen?'

'What for?'

'Rent.'

'Nothing. I didn't have to pay him rent.'

'Ah, so how did you have to pay him?'

'Pay him for what?'

'For staying there? Did you give him a percentage of what you earned?'

'No. I wasn't working when I lived with Stephen. I stayed at home most of the time.'

'So what did you do for money?'

'What for?'

'Buying clothes. Makeup.'

'Stephen gave me some, sometimes. I was modelling too.'

'Did John Profumo give you money?'

'What for?'

'When you went with him.'

'No.'

'What did you do when you were broke?'

'I borrowed some money.'

'Who from?'

'A friend.'

'Always the same friend?'

'No.'

'And Stephen, what did he do?'

'I don't know.'

'And Mandy?'

'Mandy didn't mind what she did. Peter put her in a flat, and gave her a lot of money. She was very upset when he died though, because he didn't leave her anything.'

'John Profumo must have given you some money?'

'I can't remember.'

'You must remember. We've got to get to the bottom of this. Exactly where money came from, to whom it was paid, and how. It will make it possible for us to see who was in the pay of the Soviets. The security of the country is at stake, we have to unravel everything. Did John Profumo ever give you any money? At all, for any reason?'

'Well, he did once.'

Immediately, Herbert was on the alert.

'Ah! How much?'

He had his pen out again.

'Twenty pounds.'

'Because you slept with him?'

'No. For my mother.'

'He gave it to you, though.'

'Yes.'

'After intercourse.'

'No. He wanted me to have something. I told him I didn't want anything. We had been talking about my family. They're only ordinary people you know, struggling along. So he left me twenty pounds saying I could give it to my mother.'

'Did you?'

'Yes.'

Reluctantly Herbert noted that Mr Profumo had given Christine Keeler twenty pounds ... 'for her mother', instead of, as he had hoped, 'after intercourse'.

'Now, this friend who gave you money?'

'Which one?'

'There were a number?'

'Some people lent me money, yes.'

'Did you pay it back?'

'Yes.'

'Always?'

'I think so.'

'The money this "friend",' Herbert sneered, 'gave you for going to America . . .?'

'No, I didn't pay that back. I was engaged to him.'

'This was Michael.'

'That's right.'

'What was his surname?'

'He wasn't anything to do with Russia or anything. He had never met any of them.' I was nearly in tears. I wasn't going to let them trap all my friends in their sordid net.

'You had other friends who gave you money?'

'Yes.'

'You must remember their names.'

Herbert was losing his temper. I had been there for hours in the cold without so much as a cup of tea.

'There was a Mr Eylan,' I said, hoping another name would get me home.

'Ah, who was he?'

'A friend.'

'And he gave you money?'

'Yes.'

'What for?'

'He liked me.'

'How much did he give you?'

'I can't remember.'

'You must remember.'

'I can't. He gave it to me quite often.'

'How often?'

'Over about two years.'

'He was your lover?'

'No. Well, I slept with him. I didn't live with him. He was – well, he was married.'

'So he came to the flat and slept with you, and gave you money?'

'Sometimes.'

'How much?'

'Twenty pounds.'

'How much did he give Ward?'

'Nothing, why should he?'

'Stephen introduced you to him?'

'No.'

'How did you meet him?'

'Through a friend of Mandy's.'

'And then you slept with him.'

'He took me out to the cinema or to dinner. Sometimes he slept with me. Sometimes he gave me money. Not always.'

'How much of the money you received from him did you give to Stephen?'

'Why?'

'You tell me.'

'Sometimes I lent Stephen some money if he hadn't got any, but it was I who always owed him.'

'Did Stephen ever ask you to meet someone who would give you money?'

'Yes,' I said, totally unaware of what Herbert was getting at.

'Ah-ha! Now we're getting to the point, Christine, aren't we?' Herbert grinned.

'What do you mean?'

'Who was this person?'

'Charles.'

'What happened?'

'We were out of cash, so Stephen suggested I went round to this man to borrow some money.'

'And you had intercourse with him?'

'No.'

'We had better continue this conversation in the morning, Christine, when you can remember your facts correctly.'

The next day they asked me the same old questions all over again. Then they let me go and I didn't see them again for a week.

20

WITNESS

LUCKY GORDON had been arrested and kept in custody until his trial, which was to open on the fifth of June. I wasn't quite as afraid as I had been of the Edgecombe trial, partly because I had been hardened by all that had happened since. It also made a lot of difference that this time I had Paula and Olive testifying with me.

Robin Drury, now my manager, came with me. Lucky pleaded innocent, which was a laugh. He was bound to go down. I had promised the other two West Indians that I wouldn't mention their names, so when I was asked whether I knew two men called Fenton and Comacchio, I answered 'No.'

I knew that these must be the West Indians, though until then I hadn't known their surnames. But because I had given them my word, I lied. I would only have involved them if I thought their evidence was needed to make sure Lucky was convicted. The one thing I didn't need was Lucky outside and after my life.

As I stepped down from the witness box, Lucky shouted:
'I have discharged counsel and want to cross-examine the witness.'

He was allowed to question me through the Judge.

'That Christine. Look, she's a prostitute and Stephen, that Stephen Ward, he was her ponce. I met her when she was pregnant . . .'

'Robin, tell them to stop him.' I pleaded.

Robin sent a note to the Judge, but it was ignored.

'She used to have men and he used to have women, and

they did it the whole time, even in front of one another. Just a prostitute – Christine. Stephen – just a ponce. Vile, filthy. They're not decent people at all . . .'

'Stop him!' I stood up and looked at the Judge, but he ignored my request.

'I tried to help her but she didn't want it. Nothing, only to carry on the horrible life of a prostitute. She even gave me VD.'

'Stop him! It's all lies. You can't let him go on with the press taking it all down!'

'Send that woman out of court.' The Judge ordered.

They were all staring at me. The Judge glared, the press, Lucky all looked. I was crying,

'Stop him, stop him!'

But a little man had come up and was leading me away. Some of the press rushed out too, in a hurry to file the story. I cried outside the courtroom.

A solicitor came up and introduced himself as Walter Lyons. Robin had asked him to come and see me.

'It's not true, what they're saying.' I told him.

He led me back into the courtroom to hear the verdict. Lucky was given three years and as he was led away past he, he hissed:

'I'll get you.'

Mr Lyons decided to have this put on record.

As we left the courtroom I went up to Burrows and Herbert, who had been watching the proceedings. In spite of the gruelling interrogations, I still felt I could trust them. Worried about having lied, I wanted to make sure that it wouldn't have affected the outcome of the trial.

'I must tell you,' I began, 'about those two names . . .'

They were clearly in a hurry to be off somewhere.

'You've got nothing to worry about. You did very well,' said Burrows, moving off.

'No, nothing to worry about.' Herbert agreed and turned away.

'But I . . .'

Lucky must have mentioned them – surely there would be trouble?

The newspapers, of course, had a field day – anything to do with me made headline news. After the trial, Robin, Mr Lyons and I went to Mr Lyons' office to look at the *News of the World* contract and the separate one Robin had made out for him to act as my manager. I was almost happy. Lucky had been put away, thank God, and it looked as though at last all my troubles were over.

I spent the evening with Robin and a friend of his called Alex. The two of them were busy looking through papers. Alex was supposed to be typing up a manuscript for the book from the tapes I had made. But they were being terribly secretive. I wondered what it was all about.

Finally they announced that they had agreed that Alex should receive £15,000 for his contribution.

'Don't bother yourself with all of this.' Robin assured me.

'Why?'

'It doesn't matter.'

'Yes, it does. I'd like to know what's going on. It's my life after all.'

Surely this man wasn't trying to get one over me too? I couldn't believe it was possible.

'I think I'll go,' I said.

'No,' Robin insisted. 'Burrows told me to look after you.'

I rang Burrows, who told me he hadn't said any such thing.

'I'm going, Robin. I won't sign anything with you. You don't tell me what's going on. And I'll take all these tapes with me. It's my story. You're trying to do something behind my back and I don't know what's going on.'

'All right. All right. We'll burn the tapes.'

Perhaps he thought I wouldn't like to see all that hard work going up in flames, but I agreed. We burnt some tapes and I left.

The contract he had tried to get me to sign gave him complete control over me. If I had wanted to get married, I would have needed his consent. If he wanted me to dance in a strip club, I would have had to do it.

Lucky appealed against the decision on 11th June. It was accepted on the grounds that the two witnesses he had tried to call, Fenton and Comacchio, had not been present. The appeal would be heard in July.

Robin said that if I gave him £10,000 he would give me back the tapes – which he carefully *hadn't* burnt – which contained evidence that I knew the two West Indians.

Ten thousand pounds. I told him in no uncertain terms what he could do with *that* idea. (I discovered later that the fine he had had to pay, for which I had lent him ninety pounds, had only been for thirty.)

Of course Lucky was appealing on fair grounds, but I couldn't see how my covering up for Fenton and Comacchio in court could matter much. After all, they would only tell the truth, and confirm my story.

* * * * *

Burrows and Herbert were still on the prowl. They wanted to know more about Stephen and the people he had introduced me to. There were more sessions at the station.

'You mentioned Charles, someone Stephen sent you to for money?'

211

'Yes.'

'What was his name?'

'Charles.'

'Where did he live?'

'Somewhere near Hyde Park, I think.'

'And his name?'

'I told you, I can't remember.'

'How often did you ask him for money?'

'Oh, I didn't. Not at all.'

'But you said you did.'

'Did I?'

'Yes. In your last statement you said you collected money from Charles.'

'I didn't. Stephen and I went round there together.'

'And after intercourse he gave you money.'

'No. No. It wasn't like that.'

'But he did give you money?'

'No.'

They dropped that.

'Now to another question, Christine.' Herbert adopted a more serious tone.

'Yes?'

'It's a very serious matter, Christine. Now you must have had an abortion since you came to London?'

'Yes, I have,' I admitted after some deliberation. Were they going to charge for that? There didn't seem any point in lying, because these two always seemed to know the answers anyway. I knew they had interviewed all my friends, everyone I had ever known. They had questioned people from every place I had worked and even visited people from back home.

'And Stephen arranged this for you?'

'No. Why should he?'

'He was a doctor.'

'He was an osteopath.'

212

'But he knew a great many doctors.'

'Maybe he did. But he didn't have anything to do with it. I wasn't even with him at the time.'

'Who did arrange it? Who performed the abortion? You must remember the name of the person.'

'Yes, I do. But I'm not going to tell you. It's nothing to do with Stephen, with spies, or with anything. I can't go around getting people into trouble.'

'You must tell us. Don't you realise how serious this is?'

'You can knock my head against a brick wall if you like. I'm not going to tell you the name. It's irrelevant.'

'You must tell us, Christine.' Herbert was menacing.

'No I won't.'

He tried another tack.

'Girls.'

'What?'

'Girls – you brought home for Stephen.'

'What do you mean?'

'You must have introduced Stephen to girls, brought girlfriends home.'

'No. Not often.'

'From the club?'

'No.'

'Where did you get the girls from, the ones you procured for Stephen?'

'Procured?'

'You found girls for Stephen?'

'Sometimes. Of course I introduced him to girls. What's wrong with that?'

'And he took them home?'

'He might have done.'

'He took them home – I suggest – and seduced them?'

'I don't know. I wasn't there. He might have done. Stephen had quite a few girlfriends. Girls liked him.'

213

'Where did he pick up the girls?'

'I don't know what you mean.'

'The girls you introduced to Stephen, where did you find them?'

'At parties, anywhere. You know. You talk to someone and then maybe introduce them to your friends. Perhaps they get on well together. Perhaps they don't.'

Burrows took a photograph from a file and showed it to me.

'Did you introduce Stephen to either of these girls?'

The picture had been taken at Cliveden, the weekend I met Jack Profumo.

'Yes. I know them. I must have introduced him to them.'

'And other girls? Where did you find other girls for Stephen?'

'Anywhere.'

'Stephen asked you to go and get him girls?'

'Not like that. Sometimes he'd say, "Look at that pretty girl. I'd like to meet her. And if I got into conversation with her, I'd introduce her to him. There's nothing wrong with that, is there?'

'The girls might think there was.'

'Why should they?'

'Being taken along . . .'

'They didn't go with Stephen unless they wanted to. Why should they?'

'This girl here, in the photograph, where did you find her?'

'At a restaurant, I think.'

'And the other one?'

'I can't remember. Is it important?'

'Yes. Very.'

'Well, I can't remember. Is there anything else you want to ask me?'

214

'Not for the moment.'

So much for spies and security. Clearly it was Stephen they were trying to make a case against. And I didn't want to answer any more of their questions. I'd lost count of the number of times I had been in that room, it must have been nearly twenty-five and I never wanted to see the faces of those two men again.

21

COURT

THE LAST, and thirtieth, time Herbert and Burrows questioned me, they arrived at Paula's flat and instead of
taking me to the station, they suggested we went into the
bedroom where we could have a 'private discussion'.

They showed me a signed statement from Mandy in
which she mentioned that an abortion had been performed
in Stephen's flat. True, there had been one; but it had
little, if anything, to do with Stephen.

'This girl's in trouble, little baby,' Stephen had told
me one day. 'Do you know of anyone who could
help?'

I didn't, but I telephoned a girl who I thought might. She
gave me another number to ring. A date was arranged and
everything was organised in the best possible way. Stephen
knew about it, that was all. The poor girl was going
neurotic. She didn't want the baby. She couldn't afford it.
She had made a mistake. She didn't have to have the baby,
and that was that.

'So you see,' Herbert explained, 'either you sign a
similar statement, or I think you will find yourself beside
Stephen in the dock.'

They were threatening to arrest me for being party
to an abortion. The facts in the statement they had
prepared for me were true. It was only how they came to be
presented in court which proved a lie. Half a fact

is often more damaging and insinuating than the full story.

* * * * *

On June 8th, Chief Inspector Herbert and Detective Sergeant Burrows arrested Stephen. He was charged on several counts, including:

'Knowingly lived wholly or in part on the earnings of the prostitution of Christine Keeler and other women contrary to Section 30 (1) of the Sexual Offences Act:'

'. . . incited Christine Keeler to procure Miss R, a girl then under the age of 21, to have unlawful sexual intercourse . . .'

'. . . knowingly lived wholly or in part on the earnings of the prostitution of Marilyn Rice-Davies and other women . . .'

'. . . conspired with other persons to procure girls under the age of 21 to have unlawful sexual intercourse . . .'

'. . . counselled and procured the commission of a felony by an unknown person, to wit the unlawful use of an instrument to procure the miscarriage of a woman . . .'

'. . . conspired with other persons to keep a brothel . . .'

'Being a male person unlawfully and knowingly lived wholly or in part on the earnings of prostitution between and including January 1st, 1963 and June 1963.'

What a laugh. I could just imagine Mandy or I saying, 'Please, Stephen, is it my turn now?'

Presumably we waited while he negotiated the price before we had it off quickly and without ceremony, in a hurry to collect our percentage from Stephen later.

'Prostitution, Christine,' Stephen had told me, 'Is a mental attitude. If you ever want to get on in this world, never choose the easy way.'

When I wanted to be a model, Stephen's advice had been: 'Don't go to bed with just anyone, for you'll only attain limited success that way. If you want to be really successful, reliability and determination are what you must have.'

What a wonderful world. Here was Robin asking me for ten thousand pounds, knowing that I had just received the twenty-three thousand from the *News of the World*. Then being forced to sign that invidious police statement, and now, on top of all that, Comacchio wanted money from me too.

This is what happened. Paula's brother had gone to the newspapers and, in return for five hundred pounds, had told them that he had hit me *before* Lucky turned up that night, and he signed a statement saying that Paula and I had lied in court over Fenton and Comacchio.

Comacchio was then offered a thousand pounds by the paper if he told the police that he had been there that night. Comacchio needed the money to pay for a barrister to defend charges that he had been living on immoral earnings in *his* forthcoming trial.

'You must help me, Christine,' Comacchio begged on the 'phone. 'I need some money. You'll have to meet me.'

I recognised the tone of voice. I had become used to blackmailers. I arranged to meet him out of town. Paula came with me and, whilst Comacchio and I talked, she sat in the car with Comacchio's aide.

'The press have offered me a thousand pounds to say I was there. If I sign the statement, I'll be sticking my neck out because the police have already been to see me about this other matter.'

'But you asked me not to mention your names. And I risked my own neck by not having you there as a witness to back me up in court.' I argued.

'But look, I'm broke and I need someone to defend me. You've got the money from the newspapers, why don't you help your friends when they're in trouble?'

'I haven't got the money yet.'

'But I need help. Look at this.' He produced a card from his pocket. On it were written the names of two policemen, Axon and Oxford, who were closely involved in the case against Stephen.

It was the first time I realised how close to the wind I was flying. Had the police themselves written the card out for Comacchio?

'Sorry, but you've got no chance of getting the money from me.'

I had had enough of this. When Comacchio's trial came up, he was found guilty and went to prison, where he agreed to sign the statement anyway. The upshot of that evening was that I asked Mr Lyons to arrange for us to meet Axon and Oxford in his office. I told the police, in a written statement, what Comacchio had threatened and how he had shown me the card.

Things had gone too far for that to make any real difference to the final outcome. Hundreds of enquiries had been made, hundreds of girls had been interviewed. There was no chance for us. We were going to be the scapegoats, to be safely locked away or thoroughly discredited so that we could never voice our opinions or reveal the truth.

At Stephen's preliminary hearing, I still hadn't grasped the full significance of what was going on, and I was the star witness. I was frightened stiff. I wasn't allowed to speak to Stephen, or to any of the other witnesses who had been grouped together. I had to stand apart.

I walked solemnly past the other witnesses. They looked such a pathetic crowd. Mandy stood out, the only decent one there. She couldn't hide the delight she felt at being suddenly the centre of attention. I felt quite the opposite. I couldn't lower my head enough for shame. The confusion and strain were too much. All these prostitutes, and Mandy and I, lumped in together as though we were part of it all. I didn't recognise any of the girls. Possibly Stephen, like any man, had taken them home for odd nights, when I wasn't around.

I appeared in the witness box and had to answer all those questions that Burrows and Herbert had asked me a thousand times before. The questions were never given in context. Combined with my brief responses, either yes or no, a distorted version of the truth came out. By the tone of voice in which the questions were put, you would have thought they had never been asked before. They weren't particularly incriminating in themselves, but this public hearing was just a taste of what was to follow.

I looked across at Stephen. He was worried and harassed, but coping. I could see the fearful strain in his eyes. I felt faint. The atmosphere in that courtroom was so heavy. Someone was going to swing all right.

I felt powerless. I was so ashamed of all this, and I didn't know how to stand up for myself. I'd had little education and just didn't know how to speak up for myself, to show what a farce it all was.

When they had finished with me, I looked towards Stephen again. He winked at me, as if to say, 'Seems all right, little baby,' but I was so upset and sad for him, that I could hardly hold back the tears as a constable led me out of court. He was a kind man and tried to comfort me. I was taken to a small room to compose myself, before being whisked away to avoid the crowds who were gathering outside.

As usual my appearance was greeted by a deathly silence. That usually lasted long enough for me to get into the building or reach the car. This time a lone voice howled from the gutter, and in one voice the crowds took up the cry, howling to yapping like hungry hounds.

'Never mind, Christine,' said Paula, pouring a cup of tea back at the flat. 'There's nothing anyone can do but live through it, and one day try and live it down.'

'Yes, I know.' But I didn't at all.

After the preliminary hearing, Stephen was granted bail. Paul Mann, who had returned from Spain, came round to see me.

'I've seen Stephen,' he told me.

'How is he?'

'Oh – he's fine.'

'Is there anything he wants me to do?'

'Well . . .' Paul paused. 'Why don't you see him?'

'Do you think I should?'

'He told me to tell you,' said Paul quickly, 'that if you don't put the blame on the police, he'll get you as far as the Lucky Gordon case is concerned.'

'What? I don't believe you. He didn't really say that?'

'Yes, he did. Come and see him. I'm just going there now.'

Paul didn't have a car with him, so I gave him a lift to Green Street, where Stephen was staying. There was something even shadier about Paul these days, and I didn't trust him.

'Are you coming in?' he asked when we arrived.

'No, I can't. I've got to go.'

'Oh, come on.'

'No. I'll be in trouble if I'm late.' I couldn't face Stephen. Not knowing what he might have been involved with was bad enough, but I couldn't cope with him threatening to 'get me'.

221

Just then, Stephen pulled up in his car. He came over to mine.

'Hello, baby.'

He looked dreadful. I didn't know what to say. The tears welled up and I drove quickly off. The tears poured down my face, so I pulled up in a side street to wipe my eyes, so that I could see the road.

'You can't do it, Christine. You can only tell the truth,' was Paula's advice. She was a very straight girl. Sensible and practical.

I couldn't figure out a way of blaming the police. What I had said in my statement was true, as far as it went. No one would have believed me if I had told them that I'd only signed the statement because the police had told me I would be charged myself if I didn't. The charges now facing Stephen were ridiculous compared to all the evidence they had about spying and security matters. In the face of that, who would take me seriously if I said I had been blackmailed over something as relatively unimportant as the abortion?

In spite of everything, I felt fairly confident Johnnie and Lucky had both been put away, even though Lucky had decided to appeal. His case was coming up in a few days. Burrows, I believed, was one of my few friends. I had sat opposite him for about two hundred hours and while Herbert got at me, Burrows brought tea and lit my cigarettes. Stephen now had really upset and angered me. How dare he look down on me like this, and think he could frighten me with threats?

Stephen's trial opened at the Old Bailey on 22nd July. The actors for this tragic farce were well cast. The witnesses for the prosecution came equipped with a barrow-load of previous convictions. The judge, Sir Archibald Marshall, was a piggy little man with a beady eye. He, at

222

least, looked as though he was enjoying himself. It has been said of him that his Puritanical upbringing made him think that anything that wasn't quite 'nice' was filthy, disgusting and revolting. Yet Stephen had come from the same kind of background. Looking at the judge, I thought he looked as though he was having the time of his life. Throughout the trial he constantly interrupted and asked impertinent questions, as though he didn't want to miss the juicy bits!

Stephen should have chosen a ferret-like defence. Instead he had a kind, gentle man, James Burge, who didn't stand a chance. Mervyn Griffith-Jones, the prosecuting barrister, by the look of him had never seen more of the world than a holiday in Jersey. He didn't look as though he had ever experienced any kind of relationship apart from those he had with clients in court, or perhaps polite teas with his wife's friends – if he had a wife. If he had sex at all, it must have been drearily, in the dark.

But he made up for his miserable existence with the sexual dramas at court. He had been involved in the *Lady Chatterley's Lover* trial – prosecuting, of course. Every word he spoke against Stephen showed his contempt. Or was his maliciousness some form of jealousy? Only a few months before, Griffith-Jones' former school chums from Eton had been reported dancing 'Knees up, Mother Brown' with their knickers down, at an old boys' reunion.

The judge, shaking hands with his colleagues that morning, had probably been shaking something quite different the night before. Yet he had the cheek to ask me at some stage during the trial whether it was conceivable that I had had intercourse with a man whose surname I didn't know.

Griffith-Jones opened for the prosecution with some fantastic allegations about the depraved life Stephen had led, and then harped on about who had introduced who to

223

whom and what for. He suggested there was a flat where we all met in groups to look through a two-way mirror at a couple, of unspecified sex, on a bed together. The mirror *had* in fact been installed in Peter Rachman's flat in Bryanston Mews, but it had been broken in 1959, long before Stephen moved in.

Griffith-Jones wandered on about brothels and ill-kept houses of pleasure. Poor man, no doubt he was having the time of his life imagining it all. Sometimes he got so carried away he had to revert back to his original point, with a quick remark about the filth and squalor, and about the evil of the act of intercourse. This evil act itself he blamed not on Adam and Eve, or even Nature – never mind God – but on Stephen Ward.

Stephen's character was thus destroyed. This was an invidious charlatan who extorted money from innocent girls, a man who sank low enough to live off immoral earnings. I wonder how much Griffith-Jones was paid for living off the earnings of immorality in court?

I stood in the witness box and swore to tell the truth, the whole truth and nothing but the truth. How very strange in a court of justice to repeat such meaningless words. Surely, if everyone told the truth, there would be no need for a Prosecution and Defence? Stranger still, since most of the other witnesses had previously sworn to the police to lie in order to protect themselves or their families from police-threatened prosecution.

The Prosecution began:

'How did you meet the defendant?'

'At Murray's Cabaret Club.'

'And after you met him, did he ask you to live with him?'

'Yes.'

'Did you then meet Mr Peter Rachman?'

'Yes.' I replied.

The seeds were sown. Peter, by now, was being exposed as the notorious landlord who used extortion to evict his slum tenants. I wasn't asked about the circumstances in which I met Peter. It was just made obvious to the jury that Peter was Stephen's friend, and that I had been introduced to him simply for the purpose of copulation. There was no mention of Sherry. I was just asked:

'Did you go and live in a flat at Bryanston Mews?'

'Yes.'

Griffith-Jones then explained how it was that Peter had visited me to have intercourse.

'Were you paid anything or given presents?' The judge piped in.

What a horrid way of putting things, I thought.

'Yes. He kept me.'

The judge seemed very annoyed. They obviously wanted to prove that I was a prostitute and I suppose in English law there is a difference between a kept woman and a prostitute, otherwise every wife in the country could be convicted. I knew the judge wanted me to say:

'Yes. He paid me every time he made love to me. In fact I wouldn't let him make love to me unless there was a certain sum left which I had agreed to beforehand, and Stephen had said "Quite right, too".'

The judge repeated his question.

'Well, yes. He kept me,' I repeated.

The judge was furious.

'So he gave you money and presents?'

'Yes.' I said, finally. I dared not say anything else.

The judge then mumbled something about the time coming when I would be warned, but the time had not yet arrived. The subject was closed, and everyone got up and went for lunch.

After lunch they tried to make out that the flat that

225

Mandy and I had shared was run by Stephen as a brothel.

'Did the defendant visit you there often?' Griffith-Jones asked.

'Yes.'

'While you were there, were you introduced to other people by him?'

I didn't realise that what he actually meant was, 'Did you have sexual intercourse with any of these people?'

'I don't remember.'

I remembered that I told the police about James Eylan, and I remembered two friends of Stephen's I had had affairs with. They had been Douglas Fairbanks Jr and Stephen's cousin. I hadn't mentioned either to the police.

'Think,' piped up the judge.

'I can't remember.'

'You must remember.'

'Perhaps a couple.'

'Were you paid for it?'

'No, I was not.' I said furiously.

They tried again.

'Did you receive money from anyone while you were living there?'

'Yes, a Mr Eylan.'

'Did you have intercourse with him?'

'Yes.'

'Who introduced you to him?'

'I met him myself.'

They dropped the subject, and went on to ask about a few other men – my Persian boyfriend and Michael.

'Who paid for the trip to America?'

'I don't remember.'

Mr Burge intervened and asked whether it was necessary to ask all these questions.

226

'We must establish whether this witness is a prostitute.' The judge explained.

He couldn't have put it plainer. I was livid.

'I would like to say,' I spoke out clearly, 'that I am not a prostitute and never have been.'

I didn't care about the consequences of speaking out of turn.

'We'll come to that later,' came the stony reply.

The questions took a new and more condemning turn.

'Did you have intercourse with Eugene Ivanov?'

'Yes.'

'Did you have intercourse with John Profumo?'

'Yes.'

'Did you have intercourse with Mr Eylan?'

'Yes.'

'Did you have intercourse with a Persian boy?'

'Yes.'

Griffith-Jones spoke with great speed, rattling off one name after the other. He relaxed. He had made his point.

They tried to make out that Stephen had suggested that I went to Mr Eylan and asked for money to give to Stephen. But I explained that this was not so. I told them I had owed Stephen a lot of money, far more than I had ever given him. He, after all, paid the rent and bills at Wimpole Mews. Very occasionally, if Stephen was short and I happened to have a few bob, I lent it to him for tea or petrol or something.

Griffith-Jones tried to establish that Stephen had been in the flat with Jack or Eugene, that Stephen had been standing round the corner, as it were, waiting for me to hand over the cash. I explained patiently that this was not so.

They were longing for me to say that I had had it off with someone in the bedroom, then pushed them out of the front door and split the spoils with Stephen. What minds they have, these barristers and judges.

Then they started on about Emil Savundra, though he wasn't named in court.

'Was this Indian Doctor supposed to pay?'

'Yes.' I said, thinking they meant pay the rent.

They asked about sex again. I said I thought he would pay for that too. They never even bothered to ask whether I had been party to this little game, so I had to tell them that I had never had sex with Savundra.

They asked me about Charles. I vaguely remembered him, but said I couldn't remember his surname. (In fact, this was the millionaire Charles Clore.) The police had twisted my evidence, but I had been too exhausted to make a fuss about changing it. As far as I could truly remember, Stephen and I had visited him once for a drink and afterwards Stephen had said to me:

'I think he fancies you. So if you're ever short of cash . . . He's very rich, you know,' and laughed.

I don't remember ever seeing Charles again. But I had told the police that I had. It was laid out, a fact in my statement. So I had to go along with it now. They suggested that Charles had given me fifty pounds, so I had gone along with that too.

'What did you do with this fifty pounds?' The prosecution demanded.

I wondered now what fifty pounds he was referring to. From modelling, or the club, or from Michael? What did I do with most of the money I got? I certainly always owed three-quarters of it. I was always borrowing money then having to pay it back.

'I repaid a loan with it.'

It was probably the truth. I don't think I've ever had fifty pounds without having to use half of it to pay someone back. Money, money, money. They talked about pounds here and pounds there as if they didn't know there was a world where whoever had the money, paid the bill of the moment. They talked as though they had never been to a restaurant where the cheque had been paid by someone else. I could just imagine Griffith-Jones and the judge at dinner together.

'Well, my dear sir. You had two cups of coffee.'

'I didn't. I only had one.'

'And then there's the tip. I'll leave three shillings and you give me the one and six.'

Again Griffith-Jones asked me what percentage of the money I made I gave to Stephen. Did they imagine Stephen and I sat down together at a desk with a calculating machine, working out percentages? The reality of our conversation about money was quite different.

'If you're going out, Christine, get some more coffee. We've run out.'

'I haven't got enough money, Stephen.'

'Well, I haven't got any cash on me either, and we must have cigarettes.'

'I'm seeing Mandy, I'll borrow a pound off her.'

And then when Mandy came round and hadn't got her taxi fare, she'd borrow a pound from Stephen or me.

'Well,' I replied. 'I usually owed him more than I ever made. I only gave him half of that.' I wondered whether Stephen had it in him to sue me for two years' rental.

Had I introduced girls to Stephen?, they enquired. Having failed to establish that Stephen procured men for me, they were turning the question round.

'Yes.'

The judge warned me that I need not answer any question that might incriminate me. Griffith-Jones assured me it didn't matter what I said, as I hadn't done anything criminal in introducing friends to Stephen. By now I didn't really care what they were harping on about.

'As far as I know,' I replied to further questions, 'some of the girls had affairs with Stephen because they liked him.'

The way they put the questions it sounded as if every girl I brought home dragged Stephen straight into the bedroom and seduced him. Maybe they wanted to prove that the girls had paid Stephen, and that I had split the winnings with him. They were mad.

After Griffith-Jones had finished with me, Mr Burge asked me some questions. He was a much kinder man. He asked whether Stephen had paid the rent. I said he had. He asked whether I was always broke. I said 'Yes.' He suggested that I could have made a lot of money as a prostitute if I had wanted to.

Then he started on the Lucky Gordon business. He asked whether I had said that Comacchio and Fenton were not present. I had expected this, and I repeated that they had not been there. Finally he asked whether I thought I owed Stephen more money than I ever paid him. I agreed that I did.

Two girls were called as witnesses after I left the witness box. One girl, who I had introduced to Stephen, told the court, clearly, that she had liked him and had had an affair with him because she wanted to. The second girl had also had an affair with Stephen and enjoyed it very much, thank you.

The next person they called was Mandy. Griffith-Jones tried to make out that Mandy had been set up by Stephen.

Again, the case rested on money. They were set on proving that our flat had been paid for in return for running a brothel with Stephen. They tried to make out that Bill Astor had paid a cheque for our rent in return for sex. Mandy explained that the cheque had been given two years before she had sex with Bill Astor, and that had been for fun.

From the way the questions were phrased, the courtroom must have imagined a load of people sitting around naked on rugs reading dirty books while Mandy and Bill performed on the sitting-room couch. That wasn't the way it was at all, of course, but it seemed that the judge couldn't comprehend even one other person being in the house while Mandy was in bed with someone. Incidentally, *I* never saw any sexy books or photos at Stephen's, despite claims to the contrary.

They asked Mandy about 'the Indian Doctor' and she admitted that he had given her money after sex, but the prosecution failed to prove that Stephen took her takings. Mandy never gave Stephen more than a quarter of the rent. In fact, Stephen was always complaining that she used the telephone far too much.

The defence tried to prove that Mandy had lied and had been pressurised into signing statements by Herbert and Burrows. She had been stopped from leaving the country once, and charged with having a fake driving licence. They kept her in Holloway for a week then. A second time she was charged with stealing a television set (it was a rented one, actually, that she had not seen since Peter Rachman's death), and she was offered bail of a thousand pounds or an easy time if she signed the statement they wanted.

It was as though the police had been ordered simply: 'Get them.' It seemed that we just had to be nicked, never mind for what or at what cost. When I learnt that Herbert had committed suicide some years later, I wondered whether he had regretted having obeyed these orders.

Next witness was 'Miss X', who guaranteed that Stephen had suggested that she perform in a bedroom where there was a two-way mirror, so that a crowd could watch from outside. But, she explained to the defence, it had been suggested as a joke.

Then Ronna Riccardo, a prostitute, came forward. Like Mandy and me, she had been pestered by the police into signing a statement. It was Herbert who had, in his own special way, explained to her that unless she signed the statements they required, her brother would be nicked for poncing, her sister would be put in a remand home, and very possibly her baby would be taken away from her. I could just imagine Herbert, saying, 'Do us a favour . . .' and keeping her at the station for hours until she would have signed almost anything.

At the preliminary hearing, Ronna had said that she and another girl had gone to bed with Stephen and another man. Now, she had new evidence. Two days before, she had made a new statement to the police and the truth was out. The judged asked whether she was saying that the police had put words into her mouth?

'Yes.'

Ronna now revealed that she had only been to Stephen's home once. They'd had a few drinks, gone to bed and that was that.

Mr Eylan – in fact, Major James Eylan – was called next. He verified what I had said, namely that Stephen had *not* introduced us but that he had given me money for going to bed with him. He also explained, which I hadn't had the chance to do, that he had known me over a long period, had taken me to restaurants and cinemas and that we were friends and didn't just see each other for the purpose of making love.

It didn't seem as though the prosecution were making much headway. Then they produced a dreadful girl. I had certainly never met her, but Stephen obviously had during that time at Bryanston Mews. Her name was Vickie Barrett and she produced the most unbelievable evidence. She was a prostitute and had been picked up by the police in Notting Hill Gate, then immediately handed over to Herbert when it was discovered that she had met Stephen once or twice.

She told the court that Stephen had picked her up in Oxford Street and had taken her home to satisfy the sexual appetite of his friends. Vickie didn't seem to know who these friends were, but they were apparently always to be found on freezing cold winter nights, lying naked on Stephen's bed, waiting to be whipped, or whatever, by Vickie.

She told the court how Stephen had been paid by these friends, that he had kept the money for her in a little drawer until it piled up. She then said that she wasn't a prostitute, although she had been caught soliciting only a year or so earlier. She described Stephen handing out horsewhips, canes, contraceptives and coffee. Having collected the utensils she would then dash into the bedroom, and the waiting client.

Vickie Barrett shared a flat with another prostitute, Brenda O'Neil, who subsequently appeared in the witness box. She too described how she had visited Stephen's flat to do business with him, but by no means on the same basis that Vickie had suggested. Although she lived with Vickie, Brenda knew nothing about Vickie's bizarre relationship with Stephen. Which wasn't in the least surprising, because Vickie had lied, as any other prostitute would, if the law told her she'd have it easier if she went along with them.

When they put Herbert in the box, he used my method of answering. When he was asked whether there had been any suggestion to the witnesses that they would be in trouble if they didn't sign statements, he replied:

'I cannot recall so doing.'

They called me back to the witness box to talk about some visit to Scotland Yard that had never happened. Mr Burge wanted to prove that Stephen had taken me there for a good talking-to about drugs. The incident was a complete fabrication, based on the occasion when Stephen had called the police in after Lucky's attack.

Finally, the farce drew to a close. While the last of the witnesses were questioned, Lucky Gordon was in the process of winning his appeal on the grounds that the two witnesses might have affected the outcome of the case. News of his success came into the Old Bailey just as Griffith-Jones was making his closing speech.

Lucky's case had been supported by evidence from the tapes Robin Drury had made, in which I acknowledged the presence of two more men. So now Griffith-Jones had his chance to get at me:

'The grounds of that appeal,' he said, 'were that her evidence was not true . . . That does not of course mean to say that the Court of Appeal have found that Miss Keeler is lying.'

Yet on went the farce, hypocritically ignoring the news that I might, in this light, have been lying about *everything*, so desperate were they to get Stephen. Griffith-Jones condemned Stephen as 'a filthy fellow', a thoroughly immoral man. He accused him of deceiving my parents and enticing me away from the quiet respectability of my home to lead a life in London under his evil eye. In the same breath he made out that I was a little tart, fully aware of what I was doing.

Stephen left the court that day to die. He had nothing left to live for. There were so many people he had known who could have come forward to save him: rich people, politicians, men with dignity and responsibility. But they didn't. They ran away from him and left him alone when he needed help most of all. Because they were afraid that their tidy, affluent little lives might be opened up like a can of worms for all to see.

Lord Astor might have come forward with his wife, who Stephen had introduced to him. He didn't. Nor did any other Lords, Dukes, Princes or Politicians. They didn't want to admit an association that wasn't quite 'nice'. So they stayed away, and Stephen was honourable enough not to mention their names.

For them it was as though nothing had really happened. They found a replacement Stephen Ward and installed him in a London flat and gave him a country cottage. They invited him to meet their friends, 'And bring along that pretty little thing, old boy.' And soon, business was back to normal. I was even invited by the more daring to a couple of sex orgies, with a new Master of Ceremonies, of course.

Stephen died, though. He died without ever hearing the verdict. He died from a self-administered drug overdose. He died of public opinion. Before he died, he lay in hospital in a coma for three days.

I cried all the time. I prayed for him to live. I couldn't sleep or eat. I rushed into my car to drive out into the streets away from everything. Moving and driving were my only freedom. Kim came with me. We stopped to buy the newspapers to see what the latest bulletin on Stephen had to say. I overheard a remark made by a stranger. Someone who had never even met Stephen:

'Oh, Ward. The ponce?'

By the time Kim had returned to the car with the papers, I had started to hate. A hatred that was violent and complete. A hatred that took me five years to get rid of. There were two innocent people crossing the road as I took my foot off the clutch, and I remember shouting at Kim.

'I'll kill them.'

I put my foot hard down on the accelerator and drove straight towards them. I hated them. Why should they live so they could sneer at Stephen and call me a prostitute? I drove on and on towards them. At the very last moment, I hooted and they just managed to jump clear of me.

'I'm going to drive straight into a wall, Kim. I'm going to.'

The car was gathering speed again. Kim was very frightened.

'Go on then,' she said calmly.

I didn't. I slowed down and drove home to sit alone crying in my room, hoping that Stephen might live.

My solicitor telephoned in the morning. It had been planned that I should fly to Germany to make a film called 'The Christine Keeler Story'. This was the same film that Stephen had signed me up for before the trial. I refused to go without knowing that Stephen would be all right.

'You must get out of the country, Christine or you'll be next. You'll be arrested.' My solicitor warned.

I still refused to go. Stephen's solicitor also rang to say that I should leave the country and make the film. Despite the bulletins from the hospital, which made it clear that Stephen was getting worse, his solicitor insisted that Stephen was improving. He assured me that Stephen would live and said it was essential that I do the film, that I was contracted to do so. So, I thought, you want your money from Stephen, whether he's alive or not.

Stephen died that night. When I woke the following morning, I swore I would never cry again. I swore that I would hold my head up, whatever happened, and live in the world without the help of anyone else. I wanted nothing. I cared for nothing and nobody.

22

ARREST

MY EVIDENCE on its own could not have convicted Stephen, but with Mandy's and the 'Indian Doctor' episode, it was enough, when mixed with the weight of public opinion, to clinch it. They brought a verdict of guilty on two counts: living on the immoral earnings of myself, and of Mandy. The Establishment must have heaved a great sigh that day.

Time dragged after Stephen's death. Macmillan got his Private Secretary to contact my solicitor for my help because I had said that I had not had sex with any other Conservative MP.

Lord Denning was compiling his report. I had to see him twice, taking my solicitor with me. I told him what I had told no one yet: that after his meeting with Sir Godfrey Nicholson, Stephen had been full of this information about underwater television cameras, and that he had heard that there had been two near-accidents, with missiles nearly going off. Denning's report was accurate in parts. But he misquoted me, and I think it was a fair old whitewash for the Establishment, all in all, and so do many others.

* * * * *

Eventually they came for me. I was having a bath. There was a knock at the door.

'I'm in the bath,' I shouted, 'Can you wait a moment?'

'You'd better get dressed,' a man replied.

I answered the door in my towel. It was The Law – there are times when they are just that. The Law had come for me.

'Who is it?' I called, though I knew.

'Detective Axon.'

There were three of them. Axon, Oxford and a policewoman. The telephone rang. Axon nearly fell over himself trying to get there before I did. I let him. I watched them take over.

'I arrest you, Christine Margaret Keeler . . .' he read out the charges.

The policewoman came into the bedroom whilst I tried to get dressed. The zipper on my dress got stuck and she couldn't fix it. I was half in and half out of the dress. Axon came into the bedroom to see what was holding us up and tried his hand at the zipper, but still they couldn't do it. Finally Oxford tried, and succeeded.

The press snatched photographs as we left the building and I directed the policemen to Marylebone Police Station. As soon as we arrived, I asked whether I could speak to my solicitor, but they refused permission. Instead they started asking me questions.

'You don't have to answer any questions, Christine,' Mr Lyons had told me, so I kept silent. I only repeated that I would not make any statements until I had seen my solicitor.

They locked me up and called for Mr Lyons. He tried to get me out on bail that night, but it was refused. Later Paula and Olive were brought in. Fenton was also down there in one of the cells. Half-way through the night, I decided that I must get hold of Mr Lyons again, to make sure that when he asked for bail, he asked it for all of us, including Fenton.

I banged on the cell door and shouted. Eventually a policeman came along.

'I must telephone my solicitor.'

'I can't let you out. It's not up to me.'

As he walked away, I yelled out that I hadn't been proved guilty yet. I continued banging and shouting until eventually they returned, and decided that I would be allowed to call. The police stood round listening very carefully to what I had to say. They couldn't have understood what I was getting at. All I needed to say to Mr Lyons was the phrase 'All of us on bail.'

Once out, we started working out some kind of defence. My preliminary hearing came up, and I had to sit there listening to the evidence of the men the prosecution had raked up. Fortunately for the prosecution, every man there bore a grudge against me.

Robin Drury was there with his bloody tapes, Lucky Gordon with his unrequited love, Pete Comacchio, John Hamilton-Marshall. They also called Mr Burrows. He came forward and gave his evidence. I could see the strain in his face. He looked as though he was utterly fed up with the whole dirty affair.

When Lucky gave his evidence, he managed to admit that he had hit me outside Paula's flat. Lucky was never a very good liar.

Between the preliminary hearing and the trial, it became clear that if I pleaded guilty on two counts – conspiracy to obstruct the course of justice (by not saying who were present as witnesses when Lucky attacked), and to perjury – I would be let off the other two charges: of wrongfully arresting Lucky .Gordon, and of maliciously accusing Comacchio of blackmail.

It was made clear to me that by terminating this hearing with a plea for the court's mercy, I would get six months inside. Whereas if I pleaded not guilty, the chances of me losing out on all four charges were fairly high, given that public opinion was dead against me. I couldn't imagine losing and having the likes of Lucky Gordon sue me for wrongful arrest.

'But, Mr Lyons,' I argued, 'It's not fair. I didn't *do* anything wrong. I was the one Lucky attacked – as Fenton will say, so will Comacchio. Yet I have to go to prison for it.'

There was nothing for it, I had to plead guilty. Fenton was bound over for three years. He explained how his wife had been going to have a serious operation the morning after Lucky's attack and that he hadn't wanted his name associated with mine because it would have upset her. Very understandable at the time. He explained how he had considered that Lucky had been rightfully arrested and that he hadn't considered it very important for him to help the police with their enquiries.

Olive got off on a year's probation but Paula and I were sentenced. Me to nine months, Paula to six.

I was grateful to be going inside. I would be safe from Lucky, now that he was free again. I would be safe from the sharks, the blackmailers and above all from the public.

'Justice' had run its course.